WHO'S WHERE IN RECREATION EDUCATION:

A Directory of Professional Preparation Curricula
in Parks, Recreation, Leisure, and Related Areas

Sponsored by the
American Association for
Leisure and Recreation
an association of
The American Alliance for
Health, Physical Education,
Recreation and Dance

E. Taylor Ellis, Editor
University of Utah
Salt Lake City, Utah

ISBN 0-88314-224-4

PURPOSES OF THE AMERICAN ALLIANCE
FOR HEALTH, PHYSICAL EDUCATION,
RECREATION AND DANCE

The American Alliance is an educational organization, structured for the purposes of supporting, encouraging, and providing assistance to member groups and their personnel throughout the nation as they seek to initiate, develop, and conduct programs in health, leisure, and movement-related activities for the enrichment of human life.

Alliance objectives include:

1. Professional growth and development--to support, encourage, and provide guidance in the development and conduct of programs in health, leisure, and movement-related activities which are based on the needs, interests, and inherent capacities of the individual in today's society.

2. Communication--to facilitate public and professional understanding and appreciation of the importance and value of health, leisure, and movement-related activities as they contribute toward human well-being.

3. Research--to encourage and facilitate research which will enrich the depth and scope of health, leisure, and movement-related activities; and to disseminate the findings to the profession and other interested and concerned publics.

4. Standards and guidelines--to further the continuous development and evaluation of standards within the profession for personnel and programs in health, leisure, and movement-related activities.

5. Public affairs—to coordinate and administer a planned program of professional, public, and governmental relations that will improve education in areas of health, leisure, and movement-related activities.

6. To conduct such other activities as shall be approved by the Board of Governors and the Alliance Assembly, provided that the Alliance shall not engage in any activity which would be inconsistent with the status of an educational and charitable organization as defined in Section 501 (c)(3) of the Internal Revenue Code of 1954 or any successor provision thereto, and none of the said purposes shall at any time be deemed or construed to be purposes other than the public benefit purposes and objectives consistent with such educational and charitable status.

Bylaws, Article III

AALR DIRECTORY

TABLE OF CONTENTS

AALR DIRECTORY

INTRODUCTION

If organized understanding of "who is doing what" is
any indication of growth and maturity of a profession the
presence of accurate and updated directories may be an in-
dicator. Currently there is concern that we know who and
what status our collegial peers have during these times
of cutback and retrenchment. This Directory is a fourth
edition of sorts, the inaugural (1969) listing 203 institutions of higher education, with subsequent issues in
1973 with 315 schools and 1981 with nearly 500 schools.
The 1969 and 1973 directories were jointly published by
NRPA and AAHPERD, the 1981 by NRPA and this 1983 edition,
sponsored by the AALR of AAHPERD.

Emphasis here has been placed on offering a directory which is as accurate and complete as possible. The
mail questionnaire, previous correspondence to the national office and referrals from AALR district representatives
provided the basis for the listings.

This publication would not have been possible without
the generous assistance, technical help and computer support of the University of Utah, Department of Leisure
Studies. Dr. Taylor Ellis is responsible for the compilation and computerization of the information contained in
this manuscript and supervised the verification of four
year schools through catalogue comparison and phone calls.
Special thanks also go to Dr. Dale Cruse, Chair of the
University of Utah for his consistent support throughout
the project. The University of Oregon, Center of Leisure
Studies, now the Institute of Recreation Research and
Service (IR^{2}S) played a major role through the leadership
of Dr. Larry Neal in both the 1973 and 1984 issues of the
directory.

The publication was initiated in the spring of 1982.
It is the third directory produced by AAHPERD/AALR of
Curriculums in Parks and Recreation. The first and sec-

ondary directories in 1969 and 1973 were accomplished through the joint efforts of AAHPERD/AALR and NRPA. This publication updates the information available in previous directories.

The format for the directory has been maintained to provide a quick reference to institutions. The directory is divided into four sections: there are two listings, the first presents institutions by state with mailing addresses, department identification and chairs, phone numbers, population (1982/83 academic year), and available course options; the second presents a listing of the community colleges presented by state including mailing addresses, department identification, etc. The third section of the directory is a compilation of institutions by degree programs offered beginning with Masters, then Directorate and finally Doctorate. The fourth section presents institutions by options.

The purposes of the directory are threefold. First is to provide a telephone/mailing directory for professionals and second, to provide a guide to students and prospective students for education exploration in the area of parks and recreation. This is to provide a source of information for trends in changes in training emphasis, changes in where curricula are housed, and changes in student population (undergraduates/graduate).

A word of clarification: the information comes from the best source possible — people in the field. The information found here is as good as the willingness of colleagues to respond by phone or questionnaire. Regarding the "options/specializations/ emphasis areas" respondents were asked to answer according to the following definition:

AALR DIRECTORY

"a definitive area of study with
several specialized courses compli-
menting a required core of general
park/recreation classes."

Added to this directory are the categories "general recreation, general resource and general cultural arts" for
those schools moving away from the proliferation of emphasis areas, offering a more general studies program.
As in past directories of this type the compilers offer
the following disclaimer — judgment of the quality of the
programs listed is not a function of such a source since
those programs listed here have not been evaluated, representatives were merely asked to respond to a brief questionnaire. A sense of quality is built in with the
designation/recognition of those schools who are accredi-
tated by the NRPA/AALR National Council of Accreditation.
However, at this early date many qualified programs not
so designated are currently considering accreditation. An
update of such schools appears in the January issues of
Parks and Recreation and AALReporter.

Thoughts as to how this resource can be even more
helpful to you as a prospective student in this field, a
student, practicing professional or faculty member are
solicited. Please use the form in the back of the Directory or otherwise share suggestions with the Executive
Director, AALR, 1900 Association Drive, Reston, Virginia,
22091.

KEY TO ALL CODES

All NRPA/AALR accredited schools are indicated by the school name being typed in **Bold** print and screened.

Degree Abbreviations are as follows: A-Associate Arts/Sciences; C-Certificate; B-Bachelor of Arts/Sciences; M-Masters; Dir-Directorate; D-Doctorate (D.Ed., Ed.D., and Ph.D.).

Abbreviations for Options/Areas of Emphasis: G1-General Recreation Program; G2-General Resource Related Program; G3-General Cultural Arts Program; CX-Corrections; CA-Camping; CI-Campus Recreation/Intramurals; CR-Church Recreation; CU-College Union Mgt.; CO-Commerical Recreation; CE-Community School Education; ER-Employee Recreation; EI-Environmental Interpretive; FM-Facility Maintenance; FR-Forest Recreation; LE-Leisure Education; MM-Marina Aquatic Mgmt.; MU-Municipal Recreation Parks; OC-Older Citizens/Aging; OE-Outdoor Education; OR-Outdoor Recreation; PM-Park Resource Mgmt.; PP-Park Resource Planning; RX-Research; RA-Recreation Administration; RL-Recreation Leadership; SR-School Recreation; SS-Special Services (Armed Forces); TR-Therapeutic Recreation; TT-Travel/Tourism; UR-Urban Innercity Recreation; VY-Voluntary/Youth Service.

EXAMPLE OF DOCUMENT CODES AND NOTATIONS

Institution — Bold type indicates AALR-NRPA accredited.

College or Major Unit Where Program is Housed

Designated Administrator

Mailing Address

University of Utah
→College of Health
L. Dale Cruse, Chair
Dept. of Recreation and Leisure
HPER N226
Salt Lake City, UT   84112

Phone: 801-581-8547
→Degrees: A B M D 254 41/22,300←
Options: CO, PM, MU, TR

Degree Levels Offered
Undergraduate Majors—
Degree Options—

Graduate Majors
Institution Enrollment

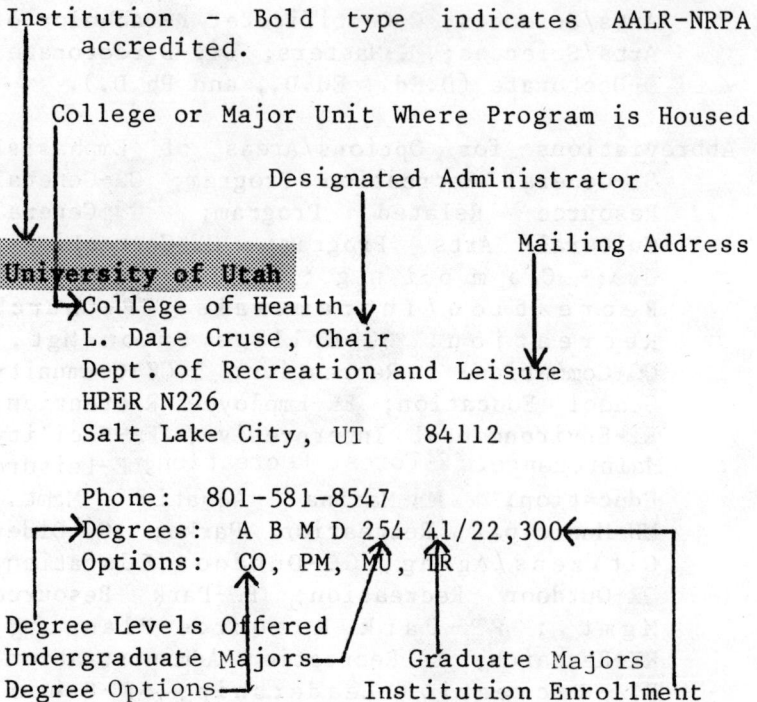

GRADUATE AND FOUR YEAR PROGRAMS

ALABAMA

Auburn University
    School of Education
    Dept. of H.P.E.R.
    H. Thomas Ford, Director
    Recreation Administration Program Area
    2050 Mem. Col.
    Auburn, AL   36849

    Phone: 205-826-4483
    Degrees: B 60 0/18,000
    Options: PM, RA, RL, TR-84, RA-85

University of Alabama
    College of Education
    Dept. of H.P.E. & R.
    Program Chairman
    Recreation and Park Leadership Program
    P.O. Box 1967
    Tuscaloosa, AL   35486

    Phone: 205-348-6075
    Degrees: B 30 2/17,000
    Options: MU, PM, TR

University of Southern Alabama
    College of Education
    Dept. of H.P.E.L.S.
    William F. Gilley, Chairman
    Leisure Services
    University Blvd.
    Mobile, AL   36688

    Phone: 205-460-7131
    Degrees: B M 150 25/29,000
    Options: CO, LE, MU, OE, OR, PM, PP, RA TR,
    TT

ARIZONA

Arizona State University
　　College of Public Programs
　　Dept. of Leisure Studies
　　Glenn W. Cheatham, Chair
　　Bixie Gammage Hall, Rm. 204
　　Tempe, AZ　85281

　　Phone:　602-965-7291
　　Degrees:　B M 260 52/40,000
　　Options:　CA, CO, MU, OE, PM, TR, TT, VY

Northern Arizona University
　　College of Education
　　Dept. of H.P.E.R.
　　Dr. Leo W. Haberlack, Chairperson
　　Box 6012
　　Flagstaff, AZ　86001

　　Phone:　602-523-4122
　　Degrees:　B 70 0/11,000
　　Options:　Gl, CX, CO, TR, Public

University of Arizona
　　School of Renewable Natural Resources
　　College of Agriculture
　　　Div. of Wildlife, Fisheries, Recreation
　　Resources
　　Dr. William W. Shaw
　　Natural Recreation Resources
　　Tuscon, AZ　85721

　　Phone:　602-621-7265
　　Degrees:　B M D 40 15/30,000
　　Options:　PM

ARKANSAS

Arkansas Technical University
    School of Systems Science
    Dept. of Recreation and Park Administration
    Dr. C. D. Dowell, Head
    Arkansas Tech.
    Russellville, AR   72801

    Phone: 501-968-0378
    Degrees: B 100 0/3000
    Options: EI, MU, RA

University of Arkansas
    Robert R. Ryan, Coordinator
    Recreation Program
    Men's Gymnasium
    Fayetteville, AR 72701

    Phone: 501-575-2859
    Degrees: M 0 16/15,000
    Options: G1

CALIFORNIA

California State Polytechnic Univ., Pomona
    School of Arts
    Dept. of H.P.E.R.D.
    Dr. Gus Gerson, Recreation Coordinator
    Curriculum in Recreation Admin.
    3801 W. Temple Ave.
    Pomona, CA 91768

    Phone: 714-598-4623
    Degrees: B 109 0/14,000
    Options: CO, OR, TR, CE

California State Polytechnic Univ., Pomona
    School of Agriculture
    Dept. of Park Administration

Joel Carter, Chairman
Recreation Admin. & Park Admin.
Cal. Poly. University
Pomona, CA 91768

Phone: 714-598-4168
Degrees: B 70 0/14,000
Options: CO, OR, PM, RA

California Poly. State Univ., San Luis Obispo
Human Development Education
Recreation Administration
Dr. Jim Railey, Head
Calif. Poly. State University
San Luis Obispo, CA 93407

Phone: 805-546-2050
Degrees: B 156 0/16,500
Options: G1, RA, TR

California State University, Chico
College of Education
Dept. of Recreation and Parks Management
Dr. Fred. A. Brooks, Chairman
130 AJH
Chico, CA 95929

Phone: 916-895-6408
Degrees: C B M 320 30/13,000
Options: CO, PM

California State University, Dominguez Hills
School of Education
Dr. Daniel B. Sawyer, Coordinator
Recreation
1000 E. Victoria St.
Carson, CA 90747

Phone: 213-516-3761/3922
Degrees: B 65 0/10,000
Options: G1, OC, TR-84

California State University- Fresno
    School of Health & Social Work
    Dr. Audrey M. Fagnani, Coordinator
    Recreation Administration Program
    Shaw & Maple Sts.
    Fresno, CA   93740

    Phone: 209-487-9011
    Degrees: B M 172 6/15,672
    Options: RA, TR

California State University, Hayward
    School of Education
    Dr. Susan E. Sunderland
    Dept. of Recreation and Leisure Studies
    A&E 246
    Hayward, CA   94542

    Phone: 415-881-3043
    Degrees: C B 80 0/11,000
    Options: G1, CO, TR, OR-84, COM.SER.-84

California State University, Long Beach
    School of Applied Arts and Sciences
    Dr. Marilyn R. Jensen, Chairman
    Dept. of Recreation and Leisure Studies
    1250 Bellflower Blvd.
    Long Beach, CA   90840

    Phone: 213-498-4071
    Degrees: C B M 260 50/32,000
    Options: G1

California State University, Los Angeles
    School of Fine Arts and Applied Arts
    Dr. Mel Finkenberg

Dept. of P.E. & Recreation/Leisure Studies
5151 State University Dr.
Los Angeles, CA 90032

Phone: 213-224-3216
Degrees: B M 60 20/24,000
Options: RA, RL, TR

California State University, Northridge

School of Communication & Professional
Studies
Dr. Byrne C. Fernelius, Chairman
Dept. of Recreation & Leisure Studies
18111 Nordhoff St.
Northridge, CA 91330

Phone: 213-885-3202
Degrees: B M 200 50/27,000
Options: CO, OR, TR, Children's Play &
Devel., Industrial Rec.,Leisure Services
Mgmt.

California State University, Sacramento

Health and Human Services
Dr. Shirley Kammeyer
Dept. of Recreation and Leisure Studies
6000 "J" St.
Sacramento, CA 95819

Phone: 916-454-6752
Degrees: B M 30 200/21,000
Options: EI, PM, RA, TR

Chapman College
Movement & Exercise Science
E. C. Keswick
Recreation Dept.
333 N. Glassell
Orange, CA 92666

Phone: 714-997-6757
Degrees: B 0 0/1150
Options: G1

Humboldt State University
    Division of H.P.E.R.
    Dr. Greg Simmons, Program Leader
    Recreation Administration
    Forbes Complex
    Arcata, CA   95521

    Phone: 707-826-4536
    Degrees: B 80 0/7,000
    Options: G1,   RA-84,   OR-84,   Community
    Service   and   Rec.-84,   Student   Designed
    Prog.-84

Pacific Union College
    Health, P.E. and Recreation Department
    Robert M. Reynolds, Coordinator
    Recreation Administration
    Angwin, CA   94508

    Phone: 707-965-6245
    Degrees: B - -/2030
    Options: PM, RA, TR, VY

Pepperdine University
    Seaver College, Natural Science Division
    Dr. George S. Poole, Director
    Dept. of Leisure Science
    24255 Pacific Coast Highway
    Malibu, CA   90265

    Phone: 213-456-4123
    Degrees: B - -/2,000
    Options: G1, Equestrian Ed.

San Diego State University
> College of Professional Studies & Fine Arts
> Dr. Mary Duncan, Chairperson
> Department of Recreation
> 5300 Campanile Ave.
> San Diego, CA   92182
>
> Phone: 619-265-5110
> Degrees: B M 300 5-10/32,000
> Options: OR, RA, TR

San Francisco State University
> School of H.P.E.R.
> Dr. Barbara Bates, Chair
> Dept. of Recreation and Leisure Studies
> 1600 Holloway Ave.
> San Francisco, CA   94132
>
> Phone: 415-469-2030
> Degrees: C B M 110 25/24,900
> Options: Gl, CO, MU, OR, PP, TR

San Jose State University
> Applied Arts & Sciences
> Paul Brown, Chair
> Recreation & Leisure Studies
> San Jose, CA   95192
>
> Phone: 408-577-2701
> Degrees: B M 200 50/26,000
> Options: CX, CO, MU, PM, RA, TR

University of California - Davis
> College of Agricultural and Environmental
> Science
> Environmental Planning & Management
> Dr. Seymour Gold, Master Advisor
> Park Admin. & Interpretation
> Davis, CA   95616

Phone: 916-752-6326
Degrees: B 80 0/18,000
Options: Gl, CI, CU, CO, ER, EI, FR, MU,
OE, OR, PM, PP, RA, TT, VY

University of La Verne
    La Verne College
    Dr. Dwight Hanawalt, Chair
    Recreation Leadership
    1950 3rd St.
    La Verne, CA 91750

    Phone: 714-593-3511 Ext. 215
    Degrees: B 20 -/800
    Options: Gl

University of the Pacific
    College of the Pacific
    Dept. of P.E. & R.
    Prof. Elkin Issac, Chairman
    Recreation Major
    Univ. of the Pacific
    Stockton, CA 95211

    Phone: 209-946-2471
    Degrees: C B M - -/6,000
    Options: CR, CO, ER, MU, SS, TR, TT, VY

University of Southern California
    Letters, Arts, and Sciences
    P.E. Dept.
    Dr. J. Tillman Hall
    Leisure and Recreation Services
    Los Angeles, CA

    Phone: 213-743-2710
    Degrees: B M D 35 14/25,000
    Options: CA, CI, LE, MU, OE, RX, RA, RL,
    SR, Internship

Whittier College
    Professor Hilmi Ibrahim
    Recreation and Physical Education
    Whittier College
    Whittier, CA   90608

    Phone: 213-693-0771, Ext. 367
    Degrees: B 54 0/1200
    Options: G1, LE, MU, OC

COLORADO

Adams State College
    Division of Education
    Dept. of H.P.E.R.
    Dr. Robert Buergister, Coordinator
    Recreation Liberal Arts
    Plachy Hall
    Alamosa, CO   81102

    Phone: 303-589-7404
    Degrees: B 15 0/2000
    Options: G1

Colorado State University
    College of Forestry & Natural Resources
    Dr. R. Burnell Held, Dept. Head
    Dept. of Recreation Resources and Landscape
    Architecture
    233 Forestry Building
    Ft. Collins, CO   80523

    Phone: 303-491-6591
    Degrees: B M D 265 35/17,000
    Options: CO, EI, FR, OR, PM, PP, RA, VY

Mesa College
    Social and Behavioral Science
    P.E. and Recreation
    Ted Swanson, Coordinator

Leisure and Recreation Services
P.O. Box 2647
Grand Jct., CO   81502

Phone: 303-245-3484
Degrees: B 90 0/3,000
Options: TT, MU, TR

University of Colorado
    Dr. Patrick Long, Coordinator
    Recreation Degree Program
    Campus Box 354
    Boulder,   CO 80309

Phone: 303-492-5370
Degrees: B M 200 14/7333
Options: CO, CE, OR, TR

University of Northern Colorado
    School of H.P.E.R.
    Max Shirley, Chairman
    Dept. of Recreation and Leisure Ed.
    Gunther Hall
    Greeley, CO   80631

Phone: 303-351-2596
Degrees: B M 155 25/10,000
Options: MU, OR, RA, RL, TR

CONNECTICUT

Central Conn. State University
    School Education
    Dept. of Human Services Student Center
    David A. Ross, Director
    Student Devel. in Higher Education
    New Britain, CT   06050

Phone:203-827-7335
Degrees: B M - -/11,000
Options: CU

Southern Connecticut State University
      School of Education
      Division of H.P.E.R.
      Chairman
      Dept. of Recreation & Leisure Studies
      501 Crescent St.
      New Haven, CT 06515

      Phone: 203-397-4384
      Degrees: B M 175 75/11,000
      Options: CO, OR, RA TR VY

University of Connecticut
      School of Education
      Dept. of Sports and Leisure Studies
      David Camaione, Chairman
      Recreation and Service Education
      U-39
      Storrs, CT 06268

      Phone: 203-486-4536
      Degrees: B M Dir D 50 25/25,000
      Options: Gl, MU, RA

DELAWARE

University of Delaware
      College of P.E., Athletics and Recreation
      Dir. Jack O'Neill
      Dept. of Recreation and Parks Adm.
      Newark, DE 19711

      Phone: 302-738-2259
      Degrees: B 45 -/13,000
      Options: Gl, PM, Recreation Fitness

FLORIDA

Florida International University
    School of Education
    Educational Leadership and Human Resources
    Development
    Coordinator
    Recreation and Parks Program
    Florida International Univ.
    Miami, FL 33199

    Phone: 305-554-3227
    Degrees: B M 112 23/14,000
    Options: G1, G2

Florida State University
    College of Education
    Dept. of Human Services and Studies
    Jean Mundy, Coordinator
    Leisure Services and Studies
    215 Stone Bldg.
    Tallahassee, FL 32306

    Phone: 904-644-6014
    Degrees: B M 180 12/21,000
    Options: RA, RL, TR

University of Florida
    College of H.P.E.&R.
    Dr. Paul R. Varnes, Chair
    Dept. of Recreation
    227 Fla. Gym
    Gainesville, FL 32611

    Phone: 904-392-4048
    Degrees: C B 240 0/33,000
    Options: MU, RA, TR

University of Miami
        School of Education and Allied Professions
        Dr. Thomas Miller, Chairman
        Dept. of H.P.E.R. & D.
        University of Miami
        Coral Gables, FL   33124

        Phone: 305-284-3711
        Degrees: B - -/8,000
        Options: G1

University of West Florida
        Arts & Science College
        Dr. Ben Williamson, Chairman
        Health, Leisure and Sports Dept.
        Pensacola, FL   32504

        Phone: 904-476-9500, Ext. 2595
        Degrees: B M 17 3/8,250
        Options: G1

GEORGIA

Columbus College
        School of Education
        Charles Ragsdale
        H.P.E.R.&Sports Science
        Algonquin Dr.
        Columbus GA   31993

        Phone: 404-568-2046
        Degrees: A C B 78 0/4,350
        Options: PM, TR, OR

Georgia Southern College
        School of Health, P.E., Recreation and
        Nursing
        Pamela S. Thomason, Dept. Head
        Dept. of Recreation and Leisure Services
        Landrum, Box 8073

Statesboro, GA   30460

Phone: 912-681-5462
Degrees: B M 135 15/6,800
Options: MU, OR, TR, CO, TT

North Georgia College
     Dept. of H.P.E.R.
     Dr. Perry Jones, Coordinator
     Curriculum in Recreation
     Dahlonega, GA   30597

     Phone: 404-864-3391
     Degrees: B 25 0/2,000
     Options: G1, G2

University of Georgia
     College of Education
     James R. Champlin
     Dept. of Recreation and Leisure Studies
     #1 Peabody Hall
     Athens, GA   30602

     Phone: 404-542-5064
     Degrees: B M Dir D 100 30/23,000
     Options: MU, OR, RA, TR, VY, CE

HAWAII

University of Hawaii
     College of Education
     H.P.E.R. Dept.
     Dr. Edward F. Chui, Professor
     Recreation Leadership Program
     1337 Lower Campus Rd.
     Honolulu, HI   96822

     Phone: 808-948-7606
     Degrees: B 70 0/20,000
     Options: G1

IDAHO

Northwest Nazarene College
    H.P.E.R.A. Dept.
    Elmore Vail, Head
    Recreation
    Nampa, ID 83651

    Phone: 208-467-8251
    Degrees: B 25 0/1,300
    Options: Gl

University of Idaho
    College of Forestry, Wildlife and Range
    Sciences
    Dept. of Wildland Recreation Management
    Dr. James R. Fazio,Head
    Moscow, ID 83843

    Phone: 208-885-7911
    Degrees: B M D 70 15/9,000
    Options: EI, FR, PM, PP, RA

University of Idaho
    College of Education
    Division of H.P.E.&R.
    Dr. Cal Lathen, Coordinator
    Recreation Management
    Moscow, ID 83843

    Phone: 208-885-6582
    Degrees: B 68 0/8,000
    Options: Gl, CO, TR, VY

ILLINOIS

Chicago State University
    George T. Stroia, Coordinator
    Recreation Department
    95th and King Dr.

Chicago, IL 60628

Phone: 312-995-2298
Degrees: B M 68 49/7,600
Options: Gl, CI, CE, ER, EI, OC, OR, RA,
SR, TR, VY

College of St. Francis
    Education and Human Services
    Lyle L. Hicks
    Dept. of Leisure Studies
    500 N. Wilcox
    Joliet, IL 60435

    Phone: 815-740-3417
    Degrees: B 40 0/800
    Options: Gl, CX, LE, OC, OR, RX, RA, RL,
    TR, UR

Eastern Illinois University
    H.P.E.R.
    Dr. Ewen L. Bryden, Chair
    Dept. of Recreation and Leisure Studies
    Rm. 10, McAfee Gym
    Charleston, IL 61920

    Phone: 217-581-3018
    Degrees: B 114 0/9,600
    Options: Gl

Elmhurst College
    Physical Ed./Business & Economics
    Chairman
    Recreation Admin./Business Mgmt.
    190 Prospect Ave.
    Elmhurst, IL 60126

    Phone: 312-833-4656
    Degrees: B 46 0/3,600
    Options: Gl, RA

George Williams College

Nelson E. Wieters, Division Director
Div. of Leisure & Environ. Resource Admin.
555 Thirty-first St.
Downers Grove, IL 60515

Phone: 312-964-3100
Degrees: B M 85 45/1,800
Options: CA, EI, MU, OE, OR, RA, RL, UR,

Illinois State University
College of Applied Science and Technology
H.P.E.R. & D.
Dr. Larry Belknap, Director
Recreation and Park Administration
McCormick Hall
Normal, IL 61761

Phone: 309-438-5608
Degrees: B M 200 10/20,000
Options: TT, CO, CX

Northeastern Illinois University
College of Education
Dr. John E. Waechter, Chairperson
H.P.E.R.A. Dept.
5500 N. St., Louis Ave.
Chicago, IL 60625

Phone: 312-583-4050
Degrees: B 35 0/10,000
Options: Gl

Rockford College
Division of Educ., P.E. and Recreation
Richard Bromley, Chairman
Program in Recreation Leadership
5050 East State St.
Rockford, IL 61101

Phone: 815-226-4044
Degrees: B 8-10 0/750
Options: G1

Southern Illinois University
    Agriculture
    George T. Weaver, Chairman
    Dept. of Forestry
    Carbondale, IL 62901

    Phone: 618-453-3341
    Degrees: B M 206 20/22,000
    Options: FR, OR, PM, PP, RX, Wilderness
    Mgt.

Southern Illinois University
    Dept. of Recreation
    Dr. William O'Brien, Chair
    Carbondale, IL 62901

    Phone: 618-453-3331
    Degrees: B M 200 20/24,000
    Options: TR, RA, CO

University of Illinois at Urbana-Champaign
    College of Applied Life Studies
    Dr. Joseph J. Bannon, Head
    Dept. of Leisure Studies
    104 Huff Gym
    1206 S. 4th St.
    Champaign, IL 61820

    Phone: 217-333-0105
    Degrees: B M D 240 63/34,914
    Options: CO, OR, RX, RA, TR

Western Illinois University
    Health, P.E. and Recreation
    Dr. Frank Lupton, Head
    Dept. of Recreation and Park Admin.

403 Currans Hall
Macomb, IL 61455

Phone: 309-298-1967
Degrees: B M 200 28/11,500
Options: CA, MU, OE, OR, PM, PP, RA, RL

INDIANA

Anderson College
    Dept. of P.E.
    Dick Young, Chairman
    Program in Recreation Leadership
    Anderson, IN 46012

    Phone: 317-649-9071
    Degrees: B 80-10 0/2,010
    Options: Gl

Ball State University
    College of Science & Humanities
    Dept. of Natural Resources
    Donald E. Van Meter, Chairman
    Major in Outdoor Recreation Management
    Muncie, IN 47326

    Phone: 317-285-7162
    Degrees: B M 170 25/18,300
    Options: EI, OR

Ball State University
    Teachers College
    Center for Lifelong Education
    James M. Elhenny
    T.C. Annex 1
    Munice IN 47306

    Phone: 317-285-5434
    Degrees: M D 0 25/17000
    Options: CE RX

Butler University
     College of Education
     Dean Joe Lamberti
     General Program
     4600 Sunset Lane
     Indianapolis, IN 46208

     Phone:317-283-9515
     Degrees: B M - -/2,400
     Options: Gl, G3, CA, CI, DR, CE, LE, OE, OR

De Pauw University
     College of Liberal Arts
     Thomas A. Mont
     H.P.E.R.D.
     Greencastle, IN 46135

     Phone: 317-658-4834
     Degrees: B M 15 2/2,350
     Options: G2

Huntington College
     H.P.E.R.
     Dr. Roy Doornbos, Jr., Director
     Recreation Management
     Huntington, IN 46750

     Phone: 219-356-6000, Ext. 180
     Degrees: B 42 0/ 450
     Options: Gl, OR, RA, TR

Indiana State University
     School of H.P.E.R.
     Ken R. Badertscher, Chairperson
     Dept. of Recreation and Leisure Studies
     218 Reeve Hall
     Terre Haute, IN 47809

        Phone: 812-232-6311, Ext. 5853
        Degrees: B 70 0/12,000
        Options: CA, OE, RA, TR

Indiana University
        School of H.P.E.R.
        Dr. Theodore R. Deppe, Chairman
        Dept. of Recreation and Park Administration
        HPER Building
        Bloomington, IN 47405

        Phone: 812-335-4711
        Degrees: B M Dir D 200 81/14,000
        Options: Gl, CA, CI, CU, LE, MU, OE, OR,
        PP, RX, RA, RL, TR

Purdue University
        Dr. Dale Hanson, Head
        Recreation Studies Program
        120 Lambert
        W. Lafayette, IN 47907

        Phone: 317-494-3178
        Degrees: B M D 75 10/35,000
        Options: CO, ER, FR, MU, PM, RA, RL, TT

Taylor University
        Physical Education Dept.
        George Glass, Chairman
        Recreation Leadership Major
        Upland, IN 46989

        Phone: 317-898-2751
        Degrees: B - -/1,435
        Options: Gl, RL

University of Evansville
        Lois D. Patton
        Health and P. E.
        P. O. Box 329

Evansville, IN 47702

Phone: 812-479-2847

IOWA

Drake University
    College of Education
    Dr. Ray Pugh & Gary Osborn
    Recreation and Leisure Services
    Bell Center
    Des Moines, IA 50311

    Phone: 515-271-3144 & 2748
    Degrees: B M 30 15/5,000
    Options: G1, CA, MU, OR, OE, RA, RL, TR, VY

Graceland College
    Division of H.P.E.R.
    Curriculum Coordinator
    B.S. in Recreation
    Lamoni, IA 50140

    Phone: 515-784-5315
    Degrees: B - -/1,000
    Options: G1

Iowa State University
    College of Education
    Dept. of P.E. and Leisure Studies
    Coordinator
    Leisure Studies Curriculum
    202 Beyer Hall
    Ames, IA 50011

    Phone: 515-294-4443
    Degrees: B 120 0/25,000
    Options: G1, OR, RA, TR

Iowa State University
        College of Agriculture
        Professor George W. Thomson, Chairman
        Dept. of Forestry
        Bessy Hall
        Ames, IA   50011

        Phone: 515-294-1166
        Degrees: B M Dir 15 1/24,906
        Options: FR

University of Iowa
        Liberal Arts
        Dr. Richard MacNeil, Chair
        Recreation Education
        W 618 SSH
        Iowa City, IA   52776

        Phone: 319-353-6733
        Degrees: B M 190 40/28,000
        Options: G1, RA, TR, Leisure Studies

University of Northern Iowa
        College of Education
        School of H.P.E.R.
        William Thrall, Head
        Recreation
        East Gym
        Cedar Falls, IA   50614

        Phone: 319-273-2654
        Degrees: B 150 0/12,000
        Options: TR, Community Recreation

Wartburg College
        Dept. of P.E. and Athletics
        Richard A. Walker, Chairman
        Leisure Services
        Waverly, IA   50677

Phone: 319-352-1200
Degrees: B 20 0/1,190
Options: Gl

KANSAS

Bethany College
    School of H.P.E.R.
    Dr. Jim Krob, Chairman
    Dept. of Recreation
    Lindsborg, KS   67456

    Phone: 913-227-3311
    Degrees: B 24 0/900
    Options: Gl

Emporia State University
    School of Education
    Division of H.P.E.R.A.
    Dr. William Quayle, Div. Chairman
    Recreation Administration Curriculum
    1000 Commercial
    Emporia, KS   66801

    Phone: 316-343-1200, Ext. 354
    Degrees: B - -/5,500
    Options: Gl

Kansas State University
    College of Arts/Sciences
    Dr. Don Lindley, Recreation Coordinator
    Recreation Major
    203 Ahearn
    Manhattan, KS   66506

    Phone: 913-532-6766
    Degrees: B M 80 1/17,500
    Options: MU, RA, RL, TR

Pittsburg State University
    Tom Lester, Coordinator of Recreation
    Weede Gymnasium
    Pittsburg, KS 66762

    Phone: 316-231-7000, Ext. 352
    Degrees: B M 38 2/5,500
    Options: CO, FR, OC, RA, TR

University of Kansas
    School of Education
    Dept. of H.P.E.R.
    Steve Sims, Prog. Coor.
    Recreation Education
    Robinson Center
    Lawrence, KS 66045

    Phone: 913-864-4305
    Degrees: B M 65 12/22,000
    Options: MU, OR, RA, TR

KENTUCKY

Eastern Kentucky University
    Dr. James McChesney, Chair
    Dept. of Recreation and Park Admin.
    Begley Bldg.
    Richmond, KY 40475

    Phone: 606-622-5975
    Degrees: A B M 155 12/13,600
    Options: CX, CR, EI, MU, OE, PM, RA

Morehead State University
    School of Education
    Dept. of H.P.E.R.
    Dr. Earl J. Bentley, Chairman
    Program in Recreation
    Morehead, KY 40351

Phone: 606-783-2180
Degrees: A B M 39 0/6,212
Options: G1, G2

University of Kentucky
    Dept. of Forestry
    Dr. Bart Thielges, Chairman
    Lexington, KY 40546

    Phone: 606-258-4609
    Degrees: B M Dr 120 30/26,000
    Options: FR

University of Kentucky
    College of Education
    Dr. Stan Labanowich, Coor.
    Recreation & Leisure Studies
    113 Seaton Bldg.
    Lexington, KY 40506

    Phone: 606-257-1623
    Degrees: B M 100 20/20,000
    Options: MU, TR

University of Louisville
    College of Arts & Sciences
    H.P.E.R.
    Mr. Clark Wood
    Recreation Education
    Louisville, KY 40292

    Phone: 502-588-6641
    Degrees: B 50 0/19,000
    Options: OR, Rec. Program Services

Western Kentucky University
    College of Education
    Dept. of Physical Education and Recreation
    Dr. Burch Oglesby, Dept. Head
    Recreation and Park Administration

Dipple Arena
Bowling Green, KY 42101

Phone: 502-745-3591
Degrees: B M 150 17/13,000
Options: G1, CO, MU, OR, TR

LOUISIANA

Louisiana State University
    School of H.P.E.R.D.
    Ronald J. Byrd, Director
    Recreational Studies
    Baton Rouge LA 70803

    Phone: 504-388-2015
    Degrees: M 0 10/30000
    Options: MU, CI

Louisiana Tech. University
    School of Forestry
    J. Lamar Teate, Director
    Forestry - Recreation Option
    Ruston, LA 71272

    Phone: 318-257-4985
    Degrees: B 113 0/11,000
    Options: G2, FR

Southern University and A&M College
    H.P.E.R.D.
    Clifford Seymour,Chair
    Dept. of Recreation and Leisure Services
    P.O. Box 9752
    Baton Rouge, LA 70813

    Phone: 504-771-5662 or 5932
    Degrees: B M 100 20/8,000
    Options: RA, TR, VY

MAINE

Unity College
    Ed. Raiola, Asst. Professor
    Outdoor Recreation
    RR 78, Box 1
    Unity, ME   04988

    Phone: 207-948-3131
    Degrees: B 60 0/650
    Options: G1, G2, OE, OR

University of Maine
    College of Forest Resources
    Floyd L. Newby, Acting Division Chairman
    Program in Recreation and Park Management
    247 Nutting Hall
    Orono, ME   04419

    Phone: 207-581-2850
    Degrees: B M D 80 5/10,500
    Options: EI, FR, PM

MARYLAND

Hood College
    Dept. of P.E.R. and Leisure Studies
    Ms. Hazael Taylor, Dept. Chair
    Recreation and Leisure Studies
    Frederick, MD   21701

    Phone: 301-663-3131, Ext. 204
    Degrees: B 25 0/1000
    Options: G1, MU, OR, TR

University of Maryland
    College of H.P.E.R.
    Dr. Fred Humphrey, Chairman
    Dept. of Recreation

2367 PERH Bldg.
College Park, MD 20742

Phone: 301-454-2930
Degrees: B M D 200 200/38,000
Options: CX, CA, CI, CU, CO, ER, EI, FM FR,
LE, MM, MU, OC, OE, OR, PM, PP, RX, RA, RL,
SS, TR, TT, UR, VY

MASSACHUSETTS

Boston University
    School of Education
    Counseling and Human Services
    Dr. Gerald S. Fain
    Leisure Studies Program
    605 Commonwealth Ave.
    Boston, MA 02215

    Phone: 617-353-3295
    Degrees: B M D 30 30/20,000
    Options: CI, OC, RX, TR, Human Services

Bridgewater State College
    Dept. of H.P.E.R.
    Dr. Edward A. Braun, Chair
    Bridgewater, MA 02324

    Phone: 617-697-1200
    Degrees: B M - -/4,500
    Options: Gl, OR, TR

Northeastern University
    Boston-Bouve College of Human Devel. Prof.
    Dept. of Rec. & Leisure Studies
    Dr. George Ackinson, Act. Chair
    3 Dockser Hall, 360 Huntington Hall
    Boston, MA 02115

Phone: 617-437-3163
Degrees: B M 175 10/25,000
Options: EI, OE, RA, TR

Springfield College
    Division of H.P.E.R.
    Donald Bridgeman, Chairman
    Dept. of Recreation and Leisure Services
    Springfield, MA 01109

    Phone: 413-788-3273
    Degrees: B M - -/2,700
    Options: CA, CO, EI, FR, MU, OC, OR, PM,
    RA, RL, SR, TR, TT, UR, VY

University of Massachusetts
    College of Food and Natural Resources
    Dept.   of   Landscape   Architecture   and
    Regional Planning
    William E. Randall, Ph.D., Director
    Leisure Studies and Resources Program
    109 Hills North
    Amherst, MA 01003

    Phone: 413-545-2255
    Degrees: A B 110 0/25,000
    Options: CO, ER, EI, MU, OR, PM, PP, RA,
    VY, Arboriculture/Urban Forestry

MICHIGAN

Calvin College
    Dept. of P.E. and Recreation
    Glen E. Van Andel
    Grand Rapids, MI 49506

    Phone: 616-957-6039
    Degrees: B 47 0/3,750
    Options: Gl

Central Michigan University

School of Ed. Health and Human Services
Richard J. Kirchner, Chair
Recreation and Park Administration, FI-102
Mt. Pleasant, MI   48859

Phone: 517-774-3858
Degrees: B M 275 100/16,100
Options: CO, OR, TR, Community Recreation

Eastern Michigan University
School of Education
H.P.E.R.D. Dept.
Ronald Saunders, Chairman
Recreation Administration
Ypsilanti, MI   48197

Phone: 313-487-0092
Degrees: B 60 0/20,000
Options: G1, TR

Ferris State College
School of Education
Dept. of H.P.E.R.
Dr. Garth S. McHattie, Program Coordinator
Recreation Leadership and Management
Big Rapids, MI   49307

Phone: 616-796-0461
Degrees: B 75 0/10,800
Options: CX, CO, FR, MU, OC, OR, PM, RA,
Fitness Specialist-83

Grand Valley State College
College Arts and Sciences
Dr. George MacDonald, Chairman
Dept. of P.E. and Recreation
College Landing - Field House
Allendale, MI   49401

Phone: 616-895-6611, Ext. 259
Degrees: B 10 0/6,850
Options: G1,TR-83

Hope College
    Dept. of P.E.R. and Athletics
    Gordon M. Brewer, Chairman
    Hope College - Dow Center
    Holland, MI   49423

    Phone: 616-392-5111
    Degrees: B 28 0/2,400
    Options: G1

Michigan State University
    Agriculture and Natural Resources
    Dr. Lewis W. Moncrief
    Dept. of Parks and Recreation Resources
    131 Natural Resources
    East Lansing, MI   48824-1222

    Phone: 517-353-5190
    Degrees: B M D 200 50/40,000
    Options: CX, CA, DR, CO, ER, EI, FM, FR,
    LE, MM, MU, OC, OR, PM, PP, RX, RA, RL, SR,
    TR, TT, UR, VY

Northern Michigan University
    School of Education
    Dept. of H.P.E.R., PEIF, 201E
    Dr. Dale E. Phelps, Coordinator
    Municipal Recreation
    Marquette, MI   49855

    Phone: 906-227-2130
    Degrees: B M 50 4/7,200
    Options: CI, CE, EI, MU, OR

University of Michigan
    School of Natural Resources
    Dr. Paul F. Nowak, Chair
    Behavior and Environmental Program
    1544 Dana Bldg.
    Ann Arbor, MI 48109

    Phone: 313-764-1410
    Degrees: B M D - -/-
    Options: CE, EI, LE, OC, OR, TR

Wayne State University
    Division of H.P.E.
    Charles H. Lewis, Chairman
    Dept. of Recreation and Park Services
    259 Matthaei Bldg.
    Detroit, MI 48202

    Phone: 313-577-4269
    Degrees: B M 95 80/29,775
    Options: CA, MU, OC, OR, RA, RL, TR, VY

Western Michigan University
    H.P.E.R.
    Dr. Roger Zabik
    Professional Prep. Prog. in Parks & Rec.
    Gary Physical Education Center
    Kalamazoo, MI 49008

    Phone: 616-383-4997
    Degrees: B 70 0/20,000
    Options: Gl, CA, CO, ER, MU, OE, PM, PP,
    RA, RL

MINNESOTA

Bemidji State College
    Dr. C. Edgington
    Dept. of P.E. & Recreation

P.E. Bldg.
Bemidji, MN 56601

Phone: 218-755-2768
Degrees: -
Options: Gl, EI, OR, RA, RL

St. Cloud State University
   Education
   Dept. of H.P.E.R.
   Dr. Yutaka Morohoshi, Coordinator
   Recreation Curriculum
   Hallenbeck Hall
   St. Cloud, MN 56301

   Phone: 612-255-2229/2155
   Degrees: B 120 0/10,500
   Options: Gl, RA, TR

University of Minnesota
   College of Education
   School of H.P.E.R.
   John H. Schultz, Head
   Div. of Recreation, Park & Leisure Studies
   203 Cooke Hall
   Minneapolis, MN 55455

   Phone: 612-373-4264
   Degrees: B M D 112 53/63,700
   Options: CO, ER, MU, OE, RA, TR, VY

University of Minnesota, Twin Cities
   College of Forestry
   Forest Resources Dept.
   Dr. L. C. Merriam, Coordinator
   Recreation Resources Mgt.
   1530 N. Cleveland
   St. Paul, MN 55108

Phone: 612-373-0847
Degrees: B M D 30 2/47,383
Options: G2, FR, PM, PP, RX

Winona State University
    Dept. of H.P.E.R.
    Dr. Gary Grob
    Division of Recreation and Leisure Studies
    Winona, MN 55987

    Phone: 507-457-2994
    Degrees: B 130 0/4,500
    Options: G1, CA, LE, OR, RA, RL, SR, TR

MISSISSIPPI

Alcorn State University
    Division of Education
    Dr. Grant A. Dungee, Chairman
    Recreation (General)
    Dept. of H.P.E.R.
    P.O. Box 510 ASU
    Lorman, MS 39096

    Phone: 601-877-6506/6507
    Degrees: B 30 0/2,500
    Options: G1

Mississippi State University
    College of Education
    H.P.E.R.
    Jack Mahurin, Dept. Head
    Recreation Management
    Box 5365
    Mississippi State, MS 39762

    Phone: 601-325-2963
    Degrees: B - -/12,000
    Options: CA, CI, CO, CE, ER, MU, RA,
    Recreation Mgt.-84

University of Southern Mississippi
    Charles Burchell, Chairman
    Recreation Dept.
    Southern Station, Box 5123
    Hattiesburg, MS 39406-5123

    Phone: 601-266-5575
    Degrees: B M 110 15/12,000
    Options: CI, MU, OR, PM, PP, RA, TR

MISSOURI

Central Missouri State University
    College of Education and Human Services
    Special Services Dept.
    Dr. Terry Simmons, Coordinator
    Recreation and Leisure Services Curriculum
    201 Lovinger Bldg.
    Warrensburg, MO 64093

    Phone: 816-429-4057
    Degrees: B M 85 9/9,500
    Options: Gl, CA, MU, OE, PP, RA, RL, TR

Missouri Western State College
    H.P.E.R. Dept.
    Dr. Drew Laudie, Coordinator
    Leisure Management
    4525 Downs Dr.
    St. Joseph, MO   64507

    Phone: 816-271-4493
    Degrees: B 74 0/4,000
    Options: CO, MU, OR, TR, VY, Private Health
    Spas

Northwest Missouri State University
    College of Education
    Dept. of H.P.E.R.D.
    Dr. James Herauf, Chairman

Recreation
Lanikin Gym
Maryville, MO   64468

Phone: 816-562-1307
Degrees: B 40 0/5,100
Options: TR

Southeast Missouri State University
Applied Arts and Sciences
H.P.E.R.
Dr. Loren Taylor
Recreation Dept., Parker Bldg.
Cape Girardeau, MO   63701

Phone: 314-651-2100
Degrees: B 80 0/-
Options: G1, G2, G3

Southwest Missouri State University
School of Science & Technology
H.P.E.R.
Dr. Gary G. Shoemaker
Recreation/Leisure Studies
901 S. National
Springfield, MO   65804

Phone: 417-836-5411
Degrees: B 180 0/15,500
Options: CO, MU, OE, OR, TR

University of Missouri, Columbia
College of Public & Community Services
Dr. David M. Compton, Chairman
Dept. of Recreation and Park Administration
624 Clark Hall
Columbia, MO   65211

Phone: 314-882-7086
Degrees: B M 277 30/24,500
Options: CO, OR, RA, TR

University of Missouri, Columbia
School of Forestry, Fisheries, Wildlife
Director D. P. Duncan
Recreational Forestry
Columbia, MO   65211

Phone: 314-882-6446
Degrees: B M Dir 318 76/25,000
Options: FR

MONTANA

College of Great Falls
Human Services
Bill Yeagle
P.E. and Recreation Dept.
Great Falls, MT   59405

Phone: 406-761-8210, Ext. 402
Degrees: A B 25 0/1,325
Options: Gl

Montana State University
College of Education
H.P.E.R. Dept.
Curt Shirer, Ph.D., Recreation Coordinator
Bozeman, MT   59717

Phone: 406-994-4001
Degrees: B M 60 5/11,000
Options: Gl

University of Montana
School of Forestry
Joel Meier, Director

Recreation Management
Missoula, MT 59812

Phone: 406-243-5521
Degrees: B M 100 15/9,000
Options: CA, FR, MU, OR, PM, RA, RL

NEBRASKA

Chadron State College
    Thomas P. Colgate, Chairman
    H.P.E.R. Division
    10th & Main
    Chadron, NE   69337

    Phone: 308-436-6344
    Degrees: B M 15 2/2,000
    Options: Gl, OE, RL, SR

Kearney State College
    School of Education
    Dept. of H.P.E.R.
    Donald Lackey, Head
    Recreation Leadership & Leisure and Fitness
    Management
    Kearney, NE   68849

    Phone: 308-236-4283
    Degrees: B 50 0/770
    Options: Gl, CO, ER, Corporate Fitness

Nebraska Wesleyan University
    Division Professional Education
    Dr. Irvin L. Peterson, Head - HPER
    Specialized Area of Parks and Recreation
    53rd & St. Paul
    Lincoln, NE   68504

Phone: 402-466-2371, Ext. 244
Degrees: B 68 0/1,150
Options: CA, LE, OC, OR, RA, SR, TR

University of Nebraska - Lincoln
    School of H.P.E.R.
    Dr. Ian M. Newman, Acting Director
    Recreation
    234 Mabel Lee Hall
    Lincoln, NE 68588-0143

    Phone: 402-472-3844
    Degrees: C B M D - -/26,000
    Options:

University of Nebraska - Omaha
    College of Education
    School of H.P.E.R.
    Dr. Edsel Buchanan, Coordinator
    Recreation/Leisure Studies Program
    60th & Dodge Sts.
    Omaha, NE 68182

    Phone: 402-554-2670
    Degrees: B M 140 12/15,000
    Options: CA, CI, CO, CE, ER, EI, MM, MU,
    OC, OE, OR, RL, TR, VY

Wayne State College
    Recreation Mgmt.
    Ron Jones, Div. Chair
    H.P.E.R.A.
    200 E. 10th St.
    Wayne, NE 68787

    Phone: 402-375-2200
    Degrees: B 7 0/2,400
    Options: Gl

NEVADA

University of Nevada, Las Vegas
    College of Education
    School of H.P.E.R.D.
    Dr. David L. Holmes, Coordinator
    Recreation Program
    4505 Maryland Parkway
    Las Vegas, NV 89154

    Phone: 702-739-3291
    Degrees: B 30 0/11,000
    Options: G1

NEW HAMPSHIRE

University of New Hampshire
    School of Health Studies
    Dr. Gus C. Zaso, Chairman
    Program in Recreation & Parks
    227 Hewitt Hall
    Durham, NH 03824

    Phone: 603-862-2391
    Degrees: B M 110 3/10,500
    Options: PM,   RA,   TR,   Recreation
    Programming, TT-84

NEW JERSEY

Fairleigh Dickinson University
    Leonard Dreyfuss College
    Dr. Barbara K. Keller, Director
    Division of Recreation and Leisure Services
    285 Madison Ave.
    Madison, NJ 07940

Phone: 201-377-4700, Ext. 301
Degrees: B M 61 25/2,100
Options: CO, MU, RA, TR, TT, Employee
Industrial

NEW MEXICO

Eastern New Mexico University
    College of Education and Technology
    School of H.P.E.R.
    Dr. Mel Creel, Coordinator
    Recreation Curriculum
    Portales, NM 88130

    Phone: 505-562-2237
    Degrees: B 40 0/4,000
    Options: Gl

New Mexico Highlands University
    Division of H.P.E.L.S.
    Leisure Services
    Dr. Bernice Waggoner, Chair
    Tourism, Leisure and Sport Management
    Las Vegas, NM 87701

    Phone: 505-425-7511, Ext. 492
    Degrees: B 15 0/2,400
    Options: Gl

University of New Mexico
    College of Education
    Dept. of H.P.E.R.
    Dr. E. A. Scholer, Coordinator
    Recreation Program
    112 Johnson Gym
    Albuquerque, NM 87131

    Phone: 505-277-5919
    Degrees: B M D 65 20/22,000
    Options: PM, RA, RL, TR

NEW YORK

Ithaca College
        School of H.P.E.R.
        Dept. of Recreation
        Dr. Ronald Simpson, Chair
        Ithaca, NY 14850

        Phone: 607-274-3335
        Degrees: B 125 0/48,000
        Options: CO, OE, OR, TR

Long Island University - C. W. Post Center
        School of Education
        Dept. of H.P.E.R.
        Dr. Arthur H. Mittelstaedt, Jr.
        Coordinator
        Program in Recreation Services Admin.
        Green Vale, NY 11548

        Phone: 516-299-2671
        Degrees: B 60 0/12,000
        Options: G1, G2, CO, ER, EI, FM, MU, OE,
        OR, PM, PP, RA, TR, TT

New York University
        School of Education, Health, Nursing, and
        Arts Professions
        Physical Education and Sports
        Dr. Arnold H. Grossman, Chair
        Program in Recreation and Leisure Studies
        635 East Building
        New York, NY 10003

        Phone: 212-598-3455
        Degrees: C B M D 30 140/37,500
        Options: RA, RL, TR, UR, Sport & Fitness

St. Joseph's College
    Liberal Arts and General Studies
    Ellen Zwalsky, Dept. Representative
    Recreation Dept.
    155 Roe Blvd.
    Patchogue, NY 11772

    Phone: 516-654-5700
    Degrees: B 45 0/500
    Options: TR, Community Recreation

State University of New York, Brockport
    School of Social Professions
    Health Science/Recreation & Leisure
    Dr. David Jewell, Coordinator
    Brockport, NY   14420

    Phone: 716-395-2278 or 2161
    Degrees: B 182 0/6,500
    Options: CO, ER, TR, Public/Quasi Public

State University of New York, Cortland
    Division of Professional Studies
    Dept. of Recreation Education
    Dr. Warren Bartholomew, Chair
    Park Center, SUNY, Cortland
    Cortland, NY 13045

    Phone: 607-753-4941
    Degrees: B M 300 20/6,000
    Options: OE, OR, TR, Community Recreation

NORTH CAROLINA

Appalachian State University
    Fine and Applied Arts
    H.P.E.R.
    Dr. E. Ole Larson, Chair
    Dr. Joseph F. Madden, Coordinator
    Recreation Curriculum

Appalachian State University
Boone, NC 28608

Phone: 704-262-3141
Degrees: B 120 0/10,000
Options: OR, RA

Belmont Abby College
Division of Professional Studies
Michael P. Reidy, Chairman
Dept. of Recreational Studies
Belmont, NC 28012

Phone: 704-825-3711
Degrees: B 40 0/801
Options: G1, RA

East Carolina University
Arts and Sciences
Dept. H.P.E.R.S.
Dr. Karen Hancock, Coordinator
Minges Coliseum
Greenville, NC   27834

Phone: 919-757-6484
Degrees: B 140 0/13,200
Options: CO, MU, PM, TR

Elon College
Dept. of H.P.E.R.
Prof. Paul Gaskill, Head
Recreation Administration Program
Box 2196
Elon College, NC 27244

Phone: 919-584-2319
Degrees: B 35 0/2,600
Options: CO, MU, RA

North Carolina State University
School of Forest Recreation
Dr. Roger Warren, Head
Dept. of Recreation Resources
Administration
4008 Biltmore Hall
Raleigh, NC   27650

Phone: 919-737-3276
Degrees: B M 160 35/22,300
Options: CO, ER, EI, FR, MM, MU, OE, OR,
PM, PP, RX, RA, SS, TT, VY

University of North Carolina
Arts and Sciences
H. Douglas Sessoms, Chairman
Curriculum in Recreation Administration
205 Pettigrew Hall, 058A
Chapel Hill, NC   27514

Phone: 919-962-1222
Degrees: B M 60 28/21,000
Options: Gl, RA, TR

University of North Carolina, Greensboro
School of H.P.E.R.D.
Dr. James R. Sellers, Coordinator
Recreation and Leisure Studies Division
Room 039, Rosenthall Gym
Greensboro, NC   27412

Phone: 919-379-5044
Degrees: B 100 0/10,200
Options: CO, EI, MU, OE, PM, TR, TT

University of North Carolina, Wilmington
Arts and Sciences
Dept. of H.P.E.R.
Dr. Robert Wolff, Coordinator
Recreation Mgmt.

610 S. College
Wilmington, NC 28403

Phone: 919-791-4330, Ext. 2256
Degrees: B 100 0/5,500
Options: CO, OR, TR

Western Carolina University
    School of Education and Psychology
    Dept. of H.P.E.R.
    Edward J. Kesgen, Asst. Prof.
    Recreation Leadership
    Cullowhee, NC 28723

    Phone: 704-227-7332
    Degrees: B 50 0/6,500
    Options: MU, OE, TR

Wingate College
    Division of Education and Social Sciences
    Bobby G. Bell, Div. Chairman
    Parks and Recreation Admin.
    Campus Box 3012
    Wingate, NC 28174

    Phone: 704-233-4061
    Degrees: A B 85 0/1,500
    Options: Gl

NORTH DAKOTA

North Dakota State University
    Tom Barnhart
    Dept. of H.P.E.R. & Athletics
    Fargo, ND 58105

    Phone: 701-237-7447
    Degrees: B - -/9,000
    Options: Gl

University of North Dakota
    College of Human Resource Development
    Dept. of H.P.E.R.
    Dr. Sandra Modisett, Director
    Division of Recreation
    HYSLOP Sports Center
    Grand Forks, ND   58201

    Phone: 701-777-4324
    Degrees: B M 80 3-5/11,000
    Options: RA, RL TR

OHIO

Bowling Green State University
    College of Education
    School of H.P.E.R., Room 200
    Dr. David Groves, Chair
    Division of Recreation and Dance
    Bowling Green, OH   43403

    Phone: 419-372-2395
    Degrees: B M 85 6/15,000
    Options: CI, CO, EI, MM, MU, OE, OR, RA,
    RL, VY, Performing Arts

Central State University
    College of Education
    Dept. of H.P.E.R.
    Gwendolyn D. Hawkins, Chairperson
    Recreation
    Wilberforce, OH   45384

    Phone: 513-376-6321
    Degrees: B 50 0/2,500
    Options: Gl, LE, MU, RA, RL, TR

Kent State University
    School of P.E.R.D.
    Coordinator

Recreation and Leisure Services Unit
Kent, OH 44240

Phone: 216-672-2015
Degrees: B M 240 10/18,000
Options: MU, OR, TR

Miami University - Oxford, Ohio
   H.P.E.R.
   Marjorie Price, Acting Chair
   Recreation Education & Programming
   Phillips Hall
   Oxford, OH 45086

   Phone:
   Degrees: C B M 140 37/15,000
   Options: OR, RA, SR

The Ohio State University
   College of Education, School of H.P.E.R.
   Dr. Nancy Waidwell, Coordinator
   Recreation Education
   OSU, 305 Pomerene Hall
   1760 Neil Ave.
   Columbus, OH 43210

   Phone: 614-422-2705
   Degrees: B M 200 25/80,000
   Options: OR, RL, TR

Ohio University
   College of Health & Human Services
   School of H.P.E.R.
   R. L. Dingle, Coordinator
   Recreation Studies
   Grover Center
   Athens, OH 45701

Phone: 614-594-6124
Degrees: B 200 0/17,000
Options: Gl, CA, MU, OE, OR, TR, Wilderness
Skills

The University of Akron
    College of Education
    Dept. of H.P.E.
    Tom Adolph, Head
    Outdoor Education
    302 E. Buchter Ave.
    Akron, OH   44325

    Phone: 216-375-7475
    Degrees: B M 8 38/26,580
    Options: LE, OE, UR, VY

University of Toledo
    College of Education and Allied Professions
    Dr. Steven L. Ranck, Chairman
    Recreation and Leisure Education
    2801 W. Bancroft
    Toledo, OH   43615

    Phone: 419-537-2757
    Degrees: B M 140 10/21,000
    Options: CO, PM, TR, VY

OKLAHOMA

Oklahoma State University
    Agriculture
    Dept. of Forestry
    Dr. Stanley B. Carpenter, Head
    Stillwater, OK   74078

    Phone: 405-624-5437
    Degrees: B M 114 14/23,000
    Options: G2, FR

Oklahoma State University
      College of Arts and Science
      H.P.E. & Leisure Services
      Pauline Winter, Chairperson
      Dept. of Leisure Services
      102 Colvin Center
      Stillwater, OK 74078

      Phone: 405-624-5502
      Degrees: B M D 165 25/23,054
      Options: OR RA TR

Oral Roberts University
      Arts and Sciences
      H.P.E.R.
      Dr. Paul Brynteson, Chair
      7777 S. Lewis
      Tulsa, OK 74171

      Phone: 918-495-6823
      Degrees: B 130 0/4,500
      Options: Gl, CA, CR, OE, OR, RL, TR

Southwestern Oklahoma State University
      Arts and Sciences
      Dr. Charles Hundley, Chair
      Dept. of H.P.E.R.
      100 Campus Dr.
      Weatherford, OK 73096

      Phone: 405-772-6611, Ext. 3187
      Degrees: C B M 350 100/6,000
      Options: Gl, CA, CI, CR, CE, EI, LE, MU,
      OE, OR, RA, RL, SR, TR

University of Oklahoma
      Arts and Sciences College
      H.P.E.R.
      Dr. Trent Gabert, Chairman
      Recreation

1401 ASP
Norman, OK   73071

Phone: 405-325-5211
Degrees: B M 125 20/21,000
Options: Gl, OR, PM, RA, TR

The University of Tulsa
    College of Education
    Division of H.P.E.R.
    Clinton D. Longacre, Coordinator
    Recreation Studies
    600 South College Ave.
    Tulsa, OK   74104

    Phone: 918-592-6000
    Degrees: B M 36 6/6,253
    Options: MU TR

OREGON

Oregon State University
    School of Forestry
    Dept. of Resource Recreation
    Perry J. Brown, Head
    Corvallis, OR   97331

    Phone: 503-754-2043
    Degrees: B M 125 9/17,000
    Options: EI, FR, OR, PM, PP, RX

Oregon State University
    School of Health Intrmurals and P.E.
    Dept. of Physical Education
    Dr. John Dunn, Chair
    Sports Leadership Option
    Langton Hall, 218
    Corvallis, OR   97331

Phone: 503-754-2643
Degrees: B 35 0/16,500
Options: Gl

Pacific University
Arts and Sciences
Division of Science
Kay Hilt, Asst. Professor
Therapeutic Recreation
2043 College Way
Forest Grove, OR 97116

Phone: 503-357-6151
Degrees: B 20 0/1,000
Options: Gl, TR

University of Oregon
College of Human Devel. and Performance
Phyllis Ford
Dept. of Leisure Studies and Services
180 Esslinger
Eugene, OR 97403

Phone: 503-686-3396
Degrees: B M D 150 30/16,000
Options: Gl, CA, OE, OR, RA, SR, TR, TT

PENNSYLVANIA

Cheyney State College
Division of Education
Dept. of H.P.E.R.
David T. Wirth, Chair
Degree in Recreation
Cheyney Road
Cheyney, PA 19319

Phone: 215-758-2265
Degrees: B 105 0/2,000
Options: Gl, TR

East Stroudsburg State College
School of Professional Studies
Dr. Elaine Rogers, Chairperson
Dept. of Recreation & Leisure Services
Mgmt.
East Stroudsburg, PA   18301

Phone: 717-424-3297
Degrees: B 95 0/4,000
Options: CO, OE-83

Messiah College
Dept. of H.P.E.R.
Dr. Layton Shoemaker, Chairman
Parks and Recreation
Grantham, PA   17027

Phone: 717-766-2511
Degrees: B 30 0/1,500
Options: G1

Pennsylvania State University
H.P.E.R.
Dr. Pat Farrell, Chairperson
Recreation and Parks Dept.
267 Recreation Bldg.
University Park, PA   16802

Phone: 814-865-1851
Degrees: B M D 275 35/33,200
Options: CO, EI, MU, OR, RA, TR, TT, Park
and Recreation Admin.

Slippery Rock University
Dept. of Parks and Recreation
Dr. James W. Shiner, Chair
Slippery Rock, PA   16057

Phone: 412-794-7503
Degrees: B M 400 100/4,800
  Options: CR, RM, TR, Env. Edu. Interp.
Serv.

Temple University
H.P.E.R.D.
Dr. Jerry Jordan, Chairman
Dept. of Recreation and Leisure Studies
313 Seltzer Hall
Broad & Columbia Ave.
Philadelphia, PA 19122

Phone: 215-787-8706
Degrees: B M D 170 140/30,000
Options: CA, CI, MU, OC, RA, RL, SS, TR,
UR, VY

SOUTH CAROLINA

Benedict College
Dept. of H.P.E.R.
Chairman
Degree in Recreation
Harden and Blanding Sts.
Columbia, SC 29204

Phone: 803-256-4220
Degrees: B 60 0/1,400
Options: Gl, RA, TR

Clemson University
College of Forest and Recreation Resources
Dr. Herbert Brantley, Head & Assoc. Dean
Dept. of Recreation & Park Administration
263 Lehotsky Hall
Clemson, SC 29631

Phone: 803-656-3400
Degrees: B M 220 29/11,618
Options: PM, TR, TT, Community Leisure
Services

SOUTH DAKOTA

South Dakota State University
    College of Agriculture & Biological Sci.
    Dept. of Horticulture - Forestry
    Dr. Paul E. Nordstrom, Head
    Park Management, Ag. Hall #112
    Brookings, SD   57007

    Phone: 605-688-5136
    Degrees: B 40 0/7,000
    Options: OR, PM

University of South Dakota
    School of Education
    Division of H.P.E.R.
    Dr. Gale A. Wiedow, Asst. Professor
    Recreation Curriculum
    DakotaDome, Room 202
    Vermillion, SD   57069

    Phone: 605-677-5336, 5337
    Degrees: B M 27 3/6,000
    Options: OR, PM, RA, RL, TR

Yankton College
    Physical Education
    Martha Wood, Head
    Recreation Management Major
    Yankton, SD   57078

    Phone:
    Degrees: B 30 0/300
    Options: Gl, LE, MU, RA

TENNESSEE

Memphis State University
     Dr. Mel Humphreys, Chairman
     H.P.E.R.
     Memphis,   TN 38152

     Phone: 801-454-2321
     Degrees: B M 65 20/19000
     Options: OR,TR, RA

Middle Tennessee State University
     School of Education
     Guy Penny, Head
     H.P.E.R.S. Dept.
     Murphy Center
     Murfreesboro, TN   37132

     Phone: 615-898-2147
     Degrees: B 40 0/10,400
     Options: OR, TR, Leisure Service Mgt.

University of Tennessee
     Dept. of Forestry, Wildlife and Fisheries
     Dr. Gary Schneider
     Forest Recreation Option
     Knoxville, TN   37901

     Phone: 615-974-7126
     Degrees: B M 200 60/28,000
     Options: EI, FR, PM, PP, RX

University of Tennessee - Knoxville
     College of Education
     H.P.E.R.
     Martha Peters, Chairperson
     Division of Recreation
     1914 Andy Holt Ave.
     Knoxville, TN   37996

Phone: 615-974-6045
Degrees: B M 80 15/28,000
Options: Gl, MU, RA, RL, TR

TEXAS

Baylor University
      Dept. of H.P.E.R.
      Dr. Nancy R. Goodloe
      Recreation Leadership with Emphasis in
      Church and Community Settings
      Box 397
      Waco, TX   76798

      Phone: 817-755-3508
      Degrees: B 75 0/10,000
      Options: Gl

LeTourneau College
      Division of H.P.E.R.
      Dr. Michael J. Fratzke
      Recreation Camp Administration
      Box 7001
      Longview, TX   75607

      Phone: 214-753-0231
      Degrees: B 25 0/1,037
      Options: CA, CR, RA

North Texas State University
      College of Education
      Chairperson
      Division of Recreation and Leisure Studies
      P.O. Box 13857
      Denton, TX   76203

      Phone: 817-565-2544
      Degrees: B M D 100 40/18,700
      Options: Gl, RA, TR

Southwest Texas State University
     School of Education
     Dept. of H.P.E.
     Roger H. Guthrie, Director
     Division of Recreational Administration
     San Marcos, TX   78666

     Phone: 512-245-2561
     Degrees: B 120 0/16,000
     Options: G1

Texas A&M University
     Agriculture
     Dr. Leslie M. Reid
     Dept. of Recreation and Parks
     106 Recreation and Parks Bldg.
     College Station, TX   77843

     Phone: 409-845-7323
     Degrees: B M D 145 100/36,000
     Options: G2, CO, EI, FM, MU, OR, PM, PP,
     RX, RA, TT, Marine/Coastal Rec.

Texas Christian University
     School of Education
     Dr. Gerald Landwer
     Dept. of Kinesiological Studies
     Ft. Worth, TX   76129

     Phone: 817-921-7945
     Degrees: B - -/6,881
     Options: G1

Texas Tech. University
     Arts and Sciences
     Dept. of H.P.E.R.D.
     Dr. Ralph Atkinson, Division Coordinator
     Recreation
     P.O. Box 4070
     Lubbock, TX   79404

Phone: 806-742-3335
Degrees: B M 125 -/23,000
Options: G1, G2, G3, CI, ER, MU, OC, PM,
PP, TR

Texas Women's University
    H.P.E.R.D.
    Dr. Jean R. Tague, Chairman
    Dept. of Recreation
    Box 23717, TWU Station
    Denton, TX 76204

    Phone: 817-383-2669
    Degrees: B M D - -/7,000
    Options: RA, RL, TR

UTAH

Brigham Young University
    College of Physical Education
    Dr. Jay H. Naylor, Chairman
    Dept. of Recreation Mgmt. and Youth
    Leadership
    273 C RB
    Provo, UT 84602

    Phone: 801-378-4369
    Degrees: B M 230 85/26,000
    Options: CE, OR, RA, TR, VY

University of Utah
    College of Health
    L. Dale Cruse, Chair
    Dept. of Recreation and Leisure
    HPR N226
    Salt Lake City, UT 84112

    Phone: 801-581-8547
    Degrees: C B M D 254 45/22,300
    Options: CO, MU, RA, TR

Utah State University
     College of Education
     Dept. of H.P.E.R.D.
     Craig W. Kelsey, Chairman
     Parks and Recreation Program
     UMC 70
     Logan, UT   84322

     Phone: 801-750-1510
     Degrees: B M 75 5/10,000
     Options: G1, TR-83, RA-83

Utah State University
     Forest Resource Dept.
     Richard F. Fisher, Head
     Recreation Resources
     UMC 52
     Logan, UT   84322

     Phone: 801-750-2455
     Degrees: B M D 30 11/11,000
     Options: CO, FR, OE, OR, PM, PP, RX, RA, TT

VERMONT

Green Mountain College
     Robert Riley, Chairperson
     Dept. of Leisure and Recreation
     College St., Gym Complex
     Poultney, VT   05764

     Phone: 802-287-9313
     Degrees: A B 80 0/-
     Options: G1, RL, TR

Johnson State College
     Business Mgt./Eco. Dept.
     Dr. John Pierce, Chairman
     Recreation/Leisure Services Mgt. Option
     Johnson, VT   05656

Phone: 802-635-2356
Degrees: A C B 150 0/1,000
Options: CO, EI, MU, TT, Hotel/Hospitality

Lyndon State College
     Dr. John De Leo
     Dept. of Recreation Management
     Lyndonville, VT   05819

     Phone: 802-626-9371
     Degrees: B 180 0/900
     Options: OE, OR, RA, TR, Ski Area Mgt.

Norwich University
     Dr. Wallace E. Baines
     Dept. of H.P.E.R.
     Northfield, VT   05663

     Phone: 802-485-5011
     Degrees: A B 60 0/1,600
     Options: CA, CR, CO, LE, OC, OE, OR, RA,
     RL, TR

University of Vermont
     Natural Resources
     Dr. John J. Lindsay, Chair
     Recreation Management
     355 Alken Ctr.
     Burlington, VT   05401

     Phone: 802-656-2684
     Degrees: B M 80 6/10,500
     Options: CO, EI, FR, OR, PP, RX, TT

VIRGINIA

Ferrum College
     Division of Recreation and Leisure Services
     Thomas N. Hickman, Program Coordinator
     Senior College in Leisure Services

Box 214
Ferrum, VA 24088

Phone: 703-365-2121, Ext. 121
Degrees: B 35 0/1,650
Options: G1, OR

George Mason University
    College of Professional Studies
    Dr. Mike Freed, Head
    Park, Recreation & Leisure Studies
    1400 University Dr.
    Fairfax, VA 22030

    Phone: 703-323-2322
    Degrees: B M 30 0/15,000
    Options: G2, Management

Longwood College
    H.P.E.R.
    Frank M. Brasile, Program Director
    Therapeutic Recreation
    Lancer Hall
    Farmville, VA 23091

    Phone: 804-392-9266
    Degrees: B 105 0/2,500
    Options: TR

Lynchburg College
    H.P.E.R.
    Dr. Aubrey Moon
    Recreation
    Lynchburg, VA 24501

    Phone: 804-522-8286
    Degrees: B 30 0/1,600
    Options: G1

Marymount College of Virginia
        Div. of Education and Human Services
        Liane M. Summerfield, Coordinator
        Program in Recreation & Fitness Mgt.
        2807 N. Glebe Rd.
        Arlington, VA 22207

        Phone: 703-522-5600, Ext. 356
        Degrees: A B 25 0/1,100
        Options: CO, ER, Physical Fitness Prog.

Old Dominion University
        Darden School of Education
        Division of H.P.E.R.
        Stephen G. Greiner
        Leisure Studies & Services
        Norfolk, VA 23508-8502

        Phone: 804-440-3344
        Degrees: B 100 0/15,000
        Options: CO, OR, RA, TR

Radford University
        School of Business and Professional Studies
        Dr. Gerald S. O'Morrow, Chair
        Dept. of Recreation and Leisure Services
        Box 5736
        Radford, VA 24142

        Phone: 703-731-5221
        Degrees: B M 126 8/5,556
        Options: CA, CI, MU, OE, OR, RA, RL, TR

Shenendoah College
        Bess Wood, Chairman
        Dept. of P.E.R.(Therapeutic)
        Winchester, VA 22611

Phone: 703-667-8714
Degrees: B 17 0/805
Options: TR

Virginia Commonwealth University
School of Comm. & Public Affairs
Dr. Charles E. Hartsoe, Chairman
Dept. of Recreation
923 West Franklin St.
Richmond, VA   23284

Phone: 804-257-1131
Degrees: B M 100 25/20,000
Options: CX, CO, ER, MU, OC, PM, PP, RX,
RA, RL, SS, TR, TT, VY

Virginia Tech.
Dept. of Forestry
J. D. Wellman, Section Coordinator
Forest Recreation and Park Mgt.
Cheatham Hall
Blacksburg, VA   24061

Phone: 703-961-6663
Degrees: B M D 20 10/20,000
Options: EI, FR, OR, PM, PP

Virginia Tech.
College of Education
H.P.E.R.
Gene A.   Hayes, Program Leader
Recreation Program
Blacksburg, VA   24061

Phone: 703-961-5743
Degrees: B M D 100 25/21,000
Options: MU, OE, TR

WASHINGTON

Central Washington University
    School of Professional Studies
    Dept. of H.P.E. & Leisure Studies
    Program Director
    Leisure Services
    206 Edison Hall
    Ellensburg, WA 98926

    Phone: 509-963-1314
    Degrees: B M 100 5/7,000
    Options: G1, G3

Eastern Washington University
    Human Learning and Development
    Dr. Howard F. Uibel, Chairman
    Dept. of Recreation and Leisure Services
    Cheney, WA 99004

    Phone: 509-359-2464
    Degrees: B M 185 5/8,200
    Options: CI, CR, CO, ER, MU, OC, OE, OR,
    PM, RA, RL, SS, TR, VY

Pacific Lutheran University
    School of Physical Education
    David M. Olson, Dean
    Recreation Concentration Degree Prog.
    Tacoma, WA 98447

    Phone: 206-535-7350
    Degrees: B 120 0/3,500
    Options: G1, CI, RL, SR, TR

University of Washington
    College of Forest Resources
    Mgt. and Social Sciences Div.
    Prof. Grant W. Sharpe

Wildland Recreation, AR-10
Seattle, WA 98195

Phone: 206-545-0884
Degrees: B M D 30 36/36,000
Options: EI, FR, OR, PM, PP, RX

Washington State University
Men's Physical Education/Recreation
Dr. Roger C. Wiley
Recreation and Leisure Studies
Pullman, WA 99164-1410

Phone: 509-335-4593
Degrees: B 150+ 0/16,500
Options: G1, G2, CO, MU, PM, TR

Western Washington University
College of Arts and Sciences
Dr. James E. Moore, Coor.
Recreation and Parks
301 Bond Hall
Bellingham, WA 98225

Phone: 206-676-3782
Degrees: B 140 0/9,600
Options: G1

WASHINGTON, D. C.

George Washington University
School of Education and Human Devel.
Dept. of Human Kinetics and Leisure Studies
Jim Brien
1817 23rd St. NW
Washington, D.C. 20052

Phone: 202-676-6280
Degrees: B M 20 55/20,000
Options: TR, TT

Howard University
    College of Liberal Arts
    Dept. of P.E. & R.
    Dr. Marshall Banks, Chair
    Div. of Leisure Studies and Recreation
    Burr Gym, 6th & Giraro
    Washington, D.C.   20059

    Phone: 202-636-7142
    Degrees: B M 16 2/12,500
    Options: OR, PM, RA, TR

WEST VIRGINIA

Alderson Broaddus College
    Social Science
    James R. Seaton
    College Hill
    Philippi, WV   26416

    Phone: 304-457-1700
    Degrees: B 30 0/1,000
    Options: RL, TR

Marshall University
    College of Education
    Dept. of H.P.E.R.
    Dr. Raymond Busbee, Head
    Park Resources and Leisure Services
    Huntington, WV   25701

    Phone: 304-696-3186
    Degrees: B 55 0/11,500
    Options: LE, PP, TR

Shepherd College
    Division of Social Science
    Dr. Charles A. Hulse, Chairman
    Dept. of Park Administration
    Shepherdstown, WV   25443

        Phone: 304-876-2511, Ext. 354
        Degrees: B 60 0/4,000
        Options: G2

West Virginia State College
        H.P.E.R. & Safety
        Dr. Richard D. Tredway
        Recreation Service
        Institute, WV 25112

        Phone: 304-766-3164
        Degrees: B 35 0/4,400
        Options: RA, TR

West Virginia University
        Agriculture and Forestry
        Division of Forestry
        Jack Coster, Director
        Recreation and Parks Management
        329 Percival Hall
        Morgantown, WV 26505

        Phone: 304-293-3722
        Degrees: B M 115 25/21,000
        Options: EI, FR, MU, PM, PP, RA, RL, TR

                        WISCONSIN
Northland College
        Dept. of P.E. and Outdoor Education
        Grant Herman, Coordinator
        Outdoor Education
        Northland College
        Ashland, WI 54806

        Phone: 715-682-4531, Ext. 327
        Degrees: B 25 0/700
        Options: EI, OE, OR

University of Wisconsin, Eau Claire
    Dr. William B. Harris
    Hilltop Center
    Eau Claire, WI   54701

    Phone: 715-836-4757

University of Wisconsin-Green Bay
    School of Professional Studies
    Chair
    Professional Program in Recreation
    Resources
    106C Phoenix Sports Center, UWGB
    Green Bay, WI 54302

    Phone: 414-465-2069
    Degrees: B 25 0/4,500
    Options: CU, EI, TR

University of Wisconsin - La Crosse
    College of H.P.E.R.
    Dr. Ernest C. Hartmann, Chairperson
    Dept. of Recreation and Parks
    129 Wittich Hall
    La Crosse, WI   54601

    Phone: 608-785-8207
    Degrees: B M 434 156/8,659
    Options: PM, RA, RL, TR

University of Wisconsin - Madison
    College of Agriculture and Life Sciences
    School of Natural Resources
    Dr. Ron Giese, Head
    Program - Recreation Resource Management
    240 Ag. Hall
    Madison, WI   53706

Phone: 608
Degrees: B M D 90 20/43,000
Options: CA, CO, CE, FR, MU, OC, OR, PM,
PP, RX, RA, RL, SS, TR, TT, VY

University of Wisconsin, Milwaukee
    School of Allied Health Professions
    Dept. of Human Kinetics
    Richard J. Schild, Chairman
    Recreation
    P.O. Box 413
    Milwaukee, WI   53201

    Phone: 414-963-6080
    Degrees: B M D 120 -/27,000
    Options: MU, TR, Recreational Fitness

University of Wisconsin - River Falls
    Dept. of Plant and Earth Science
    Dr. Sam Huffman, Chairman
    Park Management Program
    River Falls, WI   54022

    Phone: 715-425-3345
    Degrees: B 110 0/5,300
    Options: G2, MU, PM, PP

WYOMING

University of Wyoming
    Arts and Sciences
    Donald S. Warder, Head
    Dept. of Recreation and Park Admin.
    P.O. Box 3402
    Laramie, WY   82071

    Phone: 307-766-4185
    Degrees: B M 95 10/10,000
    Options: G1, G2, CO, EI, MU, OR, PM, PP,
    RX, RA, TT

CANADA

Red Deer College
        Dept. of P.E.R.
        Ian Reid, Coordinator
        Recreation Administration
        Box 5005
        Red Deer, Alberta, Can., T4W 5H5

        Phone: 403-342-3300
        Degrees: A B 50 0/3,000
        Options: Gl, LE, MU, OC, OR, PP, RA, RL,
        TR, VY

University of Alberta
        Dr. Tom Burton, Chair
        Dept. of Recreation Administration
        Edmonton, Alberta, Can. T6G 2H9

        Phone: 403-432-5171
        Degrees: B M 235 15/25,000
        Options: EI, MU, OC, OR, PM, PP, RX, RA, TR

University of British Columbia
        School of P.E.R.
        Dr. Eric F. Broom, Chairman
        Dept. of Recreation and Leisure Studies
        2011 West Mall, Ponderosa Annex A, UBC
        Vancouver, British Columbia, Can., V6T 1W5

        Phone: 604-228-4764
        Degrees: B 150 0/25,000
        Options: RA, TT

University of Manitoba
        P.E. and Recreation Studies
        Jack Harper, Head
        Recreation Studies
        Winnipeg, Manitoba, Can., R3T 2N2

Phone: 204-474-8785
Degrees: B 100 0/18,000
Options: OR, PP, RA, TR

University of New Brunswick
Faculty   of   Physical   Education   and
Recreation
Dr. W. W. MacGillivary, Dean
Recreation Option
P.O. Box 4400
Fredericton, N.B., Can., E3B 5A3

Phone: 506-453-4579
Degrees: B 80 0/5,000
Options: G1

Acadia University
School of Recreation and P.E.
James Bayer, Dean
Prog. in Recreation Mgmt.
Wolfville, Nova Scotia, Can., B0P 1X0

Phone: 902-542-2201, Ext. 307
Degrees: B M 160 10/3,000
Options: CA, CI, CE, FM, LE, MU, OE, OR,
RX, RA

Dalhousie University
School of Recreation, P.E. & H.
Charles Ballem, Head
Recreation Division
South St.
Halifax, Nova Scotia, Can., B3H 3J5

Phone: 902-424-2152
Degrees: B M 95 10/9,000
Options: FM, LE, MU, OC, OR, RA, RL, TR

Lakehead University
    School of Forestry
    P.E. & Outdoor Recreation
    Dr. A. J. Kayll, Director
    Thunder Bay, Ontario, Can., P7B 3R7

    Phone: 807-345-2121
    Degrees: C B M - -/-
    Options: G2

Concordia University
    Loyola Campus
    Dr. R. B. Swesburg, Director
    Recreation and Leisure Studies
    7141 Sherbrooke St. W.
    Montreal, Quebec, Can., H4B 1R6

    Phone: 514-482-0320, Local 750
    Degrees: B - -430
    Options: G1

TWO YEAR DEGREE PROGRAMS

The listing of Community of Junior Colleges has been separated in this directory for several reasons; among them include:

* Ease of finding this level of training.

* The nature of these programs--being on the "grass roots" community level with a regional commitment and corresponding mission statements. The Associate level program is often characterized by rapid changes in courses offered and the inclusion/exclusion of whole programs. It is for this reason that the AALR does not attempt to <u>endorse</u>, <u>certify</u> or in any way <u>verify</u> the following programs. They are listed for the convenience of those interested in writing or calling to find out the current status of the program.

* While there are many Junior or Community Colleges which have contacted the national office in the recent past-- we are confident that there are many more who are providing some leadership in this area. Many have not been identified with AALR, if you know of such programs please contact:

> Executive Director, AALR
> 1900 Association Drive
> Reston, VA 22091

A copy of the questionnaire appearing at the back of this directory can be filled out and mailed to Reston for inclusion in the next directory.

ALABAMA

Jefferson State Jr. College
  Division of H.P.E.R.
  Coordinator
  Recreation Leadership
  2601 Carson Rd.
  Birmingham, AL 35215

  Phone: 205-853-1200
  Degrees: A 35/6,700
  Options: G1

CALIFORNIA

Allan Hancock College
  Bob McCutchen
  Recreation Leadership
  800 S. Callepe Dr.
  Santa Maria, CA 93454

  Phone: 805-922-3481
  Degrees: A 8/4,000
  Options: RA, RL

American River College
  Larry Foxworthy
  Forestry Dept.
  4700 College Oak Dr.
  Sacramento, CA

  Phone: 916-484-8281
  Degrees: A 40/25,000
  Options: G2, EI, FM, FR, PM, PP

Antelope Valley College
  Brent Carder
  P.E. and Athletics
  Recreation

    3041 West Avenue K
    Lancaster, CA 93534

    Phone: 805-943-3241
    Degrees: A C -/6,300
    Options: Gl, CA, RL

Butte College
    Agriculture and Natural Resources Dept.
    Howard Holman, Coordinator
    Park and Recreation
    3536 Butte Campus Dr.
    Oroville, CA 95965

    Phone: 916-895-2557
    Degrees: A C 20/9,000
    Options: PM

Cabrillo College
    H.P.E.R.
    Recreation Leadership
    6500 Soquel Dr.
    Aptos, CA 95003

    Phone: 408-425-6266
    Degrees: A 23/10,000
    Options: Gl, OR, RL

California State College
    School of Natural Sciences
    Dept. of P.E.R.
    Dr. Gregory L. Price, Coordinator
    5500 St. Coll. Pky.
    San Bernardino, CA 92407

    Phone: 714-887-7563
    Degrees: Minor
    Options: --

Chabot College
      Dept. of Recreation
      Norman Olson
      Park Tech. & Recreation Leadership
      25555 Hesperian Blvd.
      Hayward, CA   94545

      Phone: 415-786-6668
      Degrees: A 100/20,000
      Options: Gl, CA, CO, CE, EI, LE, OE, OR,
      PM, PP, RL, SR, TR, TT, UR, VY

Compton Community College
      Charles Ramsey
      Recreation Education
      1111 E. Artesia Blvd.
      Compton, CA   90221

      Phone: 213-637-2660
      Degrees: A C 83/5,000
      Options: Gl

Cuesta College
      Warren E. Hansen
      P.E.
      P.O. Box J
      San Luis Obispo, CA   93403

      Phone: 805-544-2943
      Degrees: A -/3,500
      Options: Gl

De Anza   Community College
      Recreation Management Dept.
      Dr. Charles Dougherty, Head
      21250 Stevens Creek Blvd.
      Cupertino, CA   95014

Phone: 408-996-4645
Degrees: A -/21,000
Options: Gl, CO, ER, OC, OR, RL, TR

El Camino College
　　Division of P.E.
　　Dr. James Schwartz
　　Program of Recreation Leadership
　　16007 Crenshaw Blvd.
　　Torrance, CA 90506

　　Phone: 213-352-3070
　　Degrees: A 50/28,000
　　Options: Gl

Feather River College
　　H.P.E.R. Cluster
　　Intructor
　　Prog. in Recreation Leadership
　　Box 1110
　　Quincy, CA 95971

　　Phone: 916-283-0202
　　Degrees: A 10/1,100
　　Options: Gl, CO, OR, RL, TT

Fresno City College
　　Health Arts and Science Division
　　H.P.E.R. Dept.
　　Ken Dose, Chairman
　　Recreation Leadership
　　1101 E. University
　　Fresno, CA 93741

　　Phone: 209-442-4600
　　Degrees: A C 40/14,000
　　Options: Gl

Fullerton College
　　Division of P.E.R.

Hal Sherbeck, Chairman
321 E. Chapman Ave.
Fullerton, CA 92634

Phone: 714-871-8000
Degrees: A 19/19,000
Options: G1

Kings River Community College
    Landscape Agriculture & Natural Res. Dept.
    Jim Carter, Chair
    Forest/Park Technology
    995 North Reed Ave.
    Reedly, CA 93654

    Phone: 209-638-3641
    Degrees: A -/800
    Options: G2, FR

Lassen College
    Vocational-Technical Div.
    Ken Goodman, Chairman
    Dept. of Forestry/Wildland Rec. Mgmt.
    P.O. Box 3000
    Susanville, CA 96130

    Phone: 916-257-6181
    Degrees: A -/2,800
    Options: FR

Los Angeles City College
    H.P.E.R.
    Lois Stiles, Coordinator
    Recreation
    855 N. Vermont Ave.
    Los Angeles, CA 90029

    Phone: 213-669-4000
    Degrees: A 15/22,000
    Options: G1

Los Angeles Pierce Community College
     Women's P.E.
     Prof. Flo Schulman, Coordinator
     Recreation, Leisure Mgmt.
     6201 Winnetha Ave.
     Woodland Hills, CA   91371

     Phone: 213-347-0551
     Degrees: A 35/24,900
     Options: CI, CO, FR, OR, RL, TR, TT

Los Medanos College
     P.E.R.
     Vince Custodio
     Recreation Education
     2700 Leland Rd.
     Pittsburg, CA   94565

     Phone: 415-439-2181, Ext. 3337
     Degrees: A 30/1,200
     Options: Gl, CA, LE, MU, RL

Merritt College
     Health Sciences, Human Services, and P.E.
     Ron Havemann, Asst. Dean of Instruction
     Recreation and Leisure Services
     12500 Campus Dr.
     Oakland, CA   94619

     Phone: 415-536-2495
     Degrees: A 6/9,000
     Options: Gl, CA, LE, MU, OE, OR, RL

Modesto Jr. College
     Homer N. Bowen, Advisor
     Recreational Land Management
     College Ave.
     Modesto, CA   95350

Phone: 209-575-6198
Degrees: A C 20/7,000
Options: CO, MU, OR, PM, PP

Mt. San Antonio College
    Chair & Coordinator
    Forestry & Recreation
    1100 Grand
    Walnut, CA 91789

    Phone: 714-594-5611
    Degrees: A 260/23,000
    Options: G1, G2, G3, EI, FR, MU, PM, RL,
    SR, TR, UR

Napa Valley College
    H.P.E.R. & Athletics
    Joe Jennum
    2277 Napa-Vallejo, Hwy.
    Napa, CA 94558

    Phone: 707-255-2100, Ext. 303
    Degrees: A -/5,700
    Options: G1, G3

San Bernardino Valley College
    Lorraine Psczczola
    Recreation Technology
    701 S. Mt. Vernon Ave.
    San Bernardino, CA 92410

    Phone: 714-888-6511
    Degrees: A C 20/5,000
    Options: G1, LE, RL

San Diego City College
    Bob Smith, Chair
    Recreation Leadership
    14th & Russ Blvd.
    San Diego, CA 92101

Phone: 619-230-2484
Degrees: A 35/3,000
Options: RL

San Diego Community College District
William R. Cheeseman
Program in Recreation Leadership
3375 Camino del Rio, South
San Diego, CA   92108

Phone: 619-230-2094
Degrees: A 42/25,000
Options: Gl, CO, LE, OR, RL, TT

San Diego Mesa Community College
Arts & Sciences
P.E.H.R.
E. Charles Popa
Recreation Leadership
7250 Mesa College Dr.
San Diego, CA   92111

Phone: 714-230-6854
Degrees: A C 120/21,000
Options: RL

Santa Monica College
P.E. Division
Ms. Jo Kidd, Director
Recreation and Leisure Studies
1900 Pico Blvd.
Santa Monica, CA   90405

Phone: 213-450-5150
Degrees: A C 20/7,000
Options: Gl, RL, TR

Santa Rosa Junior College
Agriculture Dept.
Joel Neuberg
Forestry - Recreation

1501 Mendocino Ave.
Santa Rosa, CA 95401

Phone: 707-527-4219
Degrees: A C 50/15,000
Options: CA, CI, FM, FR

Sierra College
    Forestry Dept.
    Bob Willhite
    Forest Technology
    500 Rocklin Rd.
    Rockling, CA 95677

Phone: 916-624-3333, Ext. 295
Degrees: A C 50/4,000
Options: G2, FR, PM

Skyline College
    Divison of P.E.R.
    Mr. Andrew Ruiz, Coordinator
    Recreation Leadership Education
    3300 College Dr.
    San Bruno, CA 94066

Phone: 415-355-7000
Degrees: A 50/8,000
Options: CA, CO, FM, LE, MU, RL, TR

University of California, Riverside
    Student Affairs/Recreation
    Dr. Vince Del Pizzo
    Recreation/Intramural Sports Program
    University Ave.
    Riverside, CA 92521

Phone: 714-787-5738
Degrees: - -/13,000
Options: G1, CI, OR

CONNECTICUT

Mitchell College
      Dept. of P.E.R.
      Douglas Harnall, Chairman
      437 Pequot Ave.
      New London, CT   06320

      Phone: 203-443-2811
      Degrees: A 18/940
      Options: Gl

Post College
      Liberal Arts
      Dept. of Recreation and Leisure Service
      Dean De Leo
      800 Country Club Rd.
      Waverbury, CT   06708

      Phone: 203-755-0121
      Degrees: A C 35/1,100
      Options: Gl, RL, TR

FLORIDA

Miami - Dade Community College - North
      Division of H.P.E. & Leisure Services
      Dr. Mary Mahan, Chair
      Professional Curriculum
      11380 N.W. 27th Ave.
      Miami, FL   33167

      Phone: 305-685-4580
      Degrees: A 25/39,000
      Options: Gl, RL

GEORGIA

Clayton Junior College
      Social Science Division

Dr. Avery Harvill
Recreation
Atlanta, GA

Phone: 404-961-3465
Degrees: A 6/3,500
Options: G1

ILLINOIS

College of Dupage
    Health and Public Services
    Sevan Sarkisian, Coordinator
    Recreational Leadership
    Glen Ellyn, IL   60137

    Phone: 312-858-2800
    Degrees: A C 35/30,000
    Options: RL

Kennedy-King College
    Melanie Anewishki, Chairperson
    Dept. of Human & Developmental Services
    6800 S. Wentworth
    Chicago, IL   60621

    Phone: 312-962-3732
    Degrees: A C -/7,200
    Options: G1, CX, CO, CE, ER, LE, OC, OR,
    RL, SR, TR

Moraine Valley Community College
    Business/P.E.
    Marilyn Twining, Coordinator
    Leisure Service Career Programs
    10900 S. 88th Ave.
    Palos, Hill, IL   60465

    Phone: 312-974-4300, Ext. 416
    Degrees: A C 65/15,500
    Options: CO, EI, FM, FR, MM, MU, PM, PP,
    RL, TT

Parkland College
    Richard D. Norris
    Dept. of Recreation
    2400 W. Bradley Ave.
    Champaign, IL 61820

    Phone: 217-351-2409
    Degrees: A 65/9,200
    Options: FM, RL, TR

Rock Valley College
    Physical Education
    Prof. E. C. Delaporte, Director
    Program in Recreation Leadership
    3301 N. Mulford Rd.
    Rockford, IL 61101

    Phone: 815-654-4426
    Degrees: A 29/5,900
    Options: RL

Triton College
    Leisure and Recreation Studies Dept.
    Henry Deihl
    2000 N. 5th Ave.
    River Grove, IL 60171

    Phone: 312-456-0300, Ext. 524
    Degrees: A C 60/25,000
    Options: Gl, CA, CO, CE, OC, PM, RA, RL, TR

INDIANA

Indiana State University - Evansville
    Division of Education

James P. Brown
Dept. of Recreation
8600 University Blvd.
Evansville, IN 47712

Phone: 812-464-1898
Degrees: C 50/3,500
Options: G1

Vincennes University Jr. College
Public Service Division
Mr. Jack Eads, Chairman
Recreation and Leisure Services Prog.
Vincennes, IN 47591

Phone: 812-885-4420
Degrees: A 60/4,500
Options: G1, CA, CI, CO, ER, FM, OC, OR,
RL, TR, VY

IOWA

Des Moines Community College
Boone Campus & Ankeny
Louis W. Alley, Chair
Recreational Leadership Program
1125 Hancock Dr.
Boone, IA 50036

Phone: 515-432-7203
Degrees: A 60/675
Options: G1

Iowa Lakes Community College
Arts and Science
Psychology, Sociology Dept.
Dan McNutt, Coordinator
Recreation Specialist Program
300 S. 18th
Estherville, IA 51334

Phone: 712-362-2604
Degrees: A 30/1,000
Options: G1

Kirkword Community College
    Dept. of Recreation & P.E.
    6301 Kirkwood Blvd.
    P.O. Box 2068
    Cedar Rapids, IA   52406

    Phone: 319-398-3549
    Degrees: A -/5,800
    Options: G1

KANSAS

Kansas City Kansas Community College
    Therapeutic Recreation Program
    Barry Baldwin, Coordinator
    7250 State Ave.
    Kansas City, KS   66112

    Phone: 913-334-1100
    Degrees: A 20/-
    Options: CX, CA, CR, OC, OE, OR, RL, SS,
    TR, VY

MARYLAND

Allegany Community College
    Dept. of P.E.R. & Athletics
    Program Director
    Recreation Leadership Curr.
    Willowbrook Rd.
    Cumberland, MD   21502

    Phone: 301-724-7700, Ext. 265
    Degrees: A 35/2,000
    Options: LE, RL

Allegany Community College
     Forestry Program
     William L. Cones, Director
     Willow Brook Rd.
     Cumberland, MD 21502

     Phone: 301-724-7700, Ext. 307
     Degrees: A 33/2,000
     Options: G2, FR

Anne Arundel Community College
     P.E.
     Skip Brown, Chairman
     General Recreation
     1091 College Parkway
     Arnold, MD 21012

     Phone: 301-269-7451
     Degrees: A 10/8,000
     Options: G1

Catonville Community College
     H.P.E.R. & Athletics
     Willa J. Brooks, Coordinator
     Dept. of Leisure Studies
     800 S. Rolling Rd.
     Baltimore, MD 21228

     Phone: 301-455-4174
     Degrees: A C 115/10,000
     Options: G1, CO, OR, TR

Montgomery College
     H.P.E.R. & Athletics
     Frank Toomey, Coordinator
     Recreation Leadership
     Montgomery College
     Rockville, MD 20850

Phone: 301-279-5218
Degrees: A 91/8,000
Options: RL

Prince George's Community College
H.P.E.R. & Athletics
Robert E. West, Assoc. Dean
Recreation Leadership
301 Largo Rd.
Largo, MD 20772

Phone: 301-322-0504
Degrees: A 20/22,000
Options: PM, RL

MASSACHUSETTS

Greenfield Community College
Behavioral Science Division
Jeanne A. Ashley, Coordinator
Program in Recreation Leadership
One College Dr.
Greenfield, MA 01301

Phone: 413-774-3131
Degrees: A 40/1,500
Options: CO, MU, OR

MICHIGAN

Grand Rapids Junior College
C. Richard Smith
H.P.E.R.
145 Bostwick Ave., NE
Grand Rapids, MI 49503

Phone: 616-456-4229
Degrees: A 35/6,000
Options: G1, G2, G3

Henry Ford Community College
        Dept. of H.P.E.R.
        Dr. Chris Kent, Head
        Recreation
        5101 Evergreen Rd.
        Dearborn, MI   48128

        Phone: 313-271-2750
        Degrees: A -/17,000
        Options: Gl, CA, RA, RL

Kalamazoo Valley Community College
        Applied Health
        Robert Sack, Coordinator
        Health, Sports & Leisure Services
        6767 West "O" Ave.
        Kalamazoo, MI   49009

        Phone: 616-372-5377
        Degrees: A -/6,800
        Options: Gl, CX, CA, CO, LE, MU, OE, OR,
        RL, TR, TT, VY

Macomb Community College
        Allied Health
        Gladys Weiss, Assoc. Dean
        Recreation Leadership
        44575 Garfield Rd.
        Mount Clemens, MI   48044

        Phone: 313-286-2047
        Degrees: A C 25/7,512
        Options: Gl, RL

Mott Community College
        P.E. Dept.,
        Fred Schutte
        Flint, MI   48502

Phone: 313-762-0450
Degrees: A 50/11,000
Options: Gl, CI, CE, LE, OE, RA, RL

Muskegon Community College
    H.P.E.R.D.
    Beth Smith, Coordinator
    Program in Recreation Leadership
    321 S. Quarterline Rd.
    Muskegon, MI 49442

    Phone: 616-777-0385
    Degrees: A 30/5,200
    Options: Gl, CX, CA, CE, MU, OR, PM, RL,
    TR, VY

MINNESOTA

Fergus Falls Community College
    H.P.E.R.
    Jerry D. Hess
    Recreation
    1414 College Way
    Fergus Falls, MN 56537

    Phone: 218-739-9670
    Degrees: A 12/600
    Options: Gl, CI, OR

Vermilion Community College
    Jon Harris, Asst. Provost
    Park and Recreation Tech.
    1900 E. Camp St.
    Ely, MN 55731

    Phone: 218-365-3256, Ext. 51
    Degrees: A 44/450
    Options: G2

MONTANA

Missoula Vocational Technical Center
    Forestry Technology Program
    William E. MacDonald, Chairman
    909 South Ave., West
    Missoula, MT 59801

    Phone: 406-721-1330
    Degrees: C 2/1,000
    Options: G2

Montana Tech
    Arts and Science Division
    H.P.E.R.
    Dr. Tom Sawyer, Head
    W. Park
    Butte, MT 59701

    Phone: 406-496-4323
    Degrees: C -/1,400
    Options: EI

NEW JERSEY

County College of Morris
    Dr. Frederick Beyer
    Recreation & Leisure Services
    Rt. 10 & Center Grove Rd.
    Randolph, NJ 07869

    Phone: 201-361-5000, Ext. 445
    Degrees: A 115/4,500
    Options: RL

NEW YORK

Orange County Community College
    Biological & Health Science Div.
    John W. Bailey, Coordinator

P.E. and Recreation Dept.
115 South St.
Middletown, NY 10940

Phone: 914-343-1121, Ext. 347
Degrees: A 35/2,400
Options: G1, OR, TR

State University of New York Agricultural and
    Technical College
    Agricultural Division
    Prof. William Bailey, Director
    Park and Recreation Management
    154 Farnsworth
    Delhi, NY 13753

    Phone: 607-746-4272
    Degrees: A 50/2,250
    Options: G1

SUNY Agricultural & Technical College
    School of Agriculture and Natural Resources
    Natural Resources Dept.
    Donald F. Jones, Dean
    Parks Management Program
    Morrisville, NY 13408

    Phone: 315-684-7083
    Degrees: A 140/2,800
    Options: FM, FR, PM, PP

SUNY School of Forestry
    Director
    Forest Technician Program
    Wanakena, NY 13695

    Phone: 315-848-2566
    Degrees: A 72/1,600
    Options: FR

Sullivan Community College
    Division of P.E.R. & Athletics
    Prof. Daniel Baldo
    Recreation Leadership
    Loch Shelorake, NY   12759

    Phone: 914-434-5750
    Degrees: A 40/1,500
    Options: G1, CO

OHIO

Hocking Technical College
    Travel and Tourism
    Business and Hospitality Mgt.
    Dr. Dean Edwards, V.P. of Instruction
    Rt. #1
    Nelsonville, OH   45764

    Phone: 614-753-3591
    Degrees: A 65/3,600
    Options: EI, FR, MU, PM, TT

Michael J. Owens Technical College
    Marion E. Michel, Chairman
    Recreational Tech.
    Oregon Rd.
    Toledo, OH   43699

    Phone: 419-666-0580
    Degrees: A 30/3,500
    Options: G1

Shawnee State Community College
    Math/Science
    Recreation and Park Management
    David E. Tedt, Coordinator
    940 Second St.
    Portsmouth,   OH 45630

Phone: 614-354-3205
Degrees: A 30/2,500
Options: EI, PM

University College
Prof. Mary Ferguson-Brown
Recreational Services Technology
Cincinnati, OH 45221

Phone: 513-475-2185
Degrees: A 75/38,000
Options: CA, CI, CO, CE, ER, FR, LE, OC,
OE, OR, RA, RL, SR, TR, VY

University of Cincinnati
College of Education
Health, PE, and Recreation
Rita M. Klenke
Program in Recreation Technology
Schmedlapp Hall, M.L. 22
Cincinnati, OH 45521

Phone: 513-475-3836
Degrees: A 35/40,000
Options: G1

OKLAHOMA

Eastern Oklahoma State College
Forest Technology Program
Ragan S. Bounds, Head
Park and Nursery Management Options
Wilburton, OK 74578

Phone: 918-465-2361, Ext. 257
Degrees: A 10/1,000
Options: EI, FM, FR, MU, OR, PM

OREGON

Clatsop Community College
    John Christie
    Forestry
    Astora, OR   97103

    Phone: 503-325-0910
    Degrees: A 15/900
    Options: FR

Southwestern Oregon Community College
    Forest Technology
    Bill Lemoine, Assoc. Prof.
    Forest Recreation
    Coos Bay, OR   97420

    Phone: 503-888-7292
    Degrees: A 40/1,800
    Options: FR, OE, OR

Umpqua Community College
    Forest Technology
    Timothy K. Gurton, Chairman
    Forest Recreation
    P.O. Box 967
    Roseburg, OR   97470

    Phone: 503-440-4600, Ext. 681
    Degrees: A 28/1,900
    Options FR, PM

PENNSYLVANIA

Harrisburg Community College
    Life Science
    William A. Nelson, Coordinator
    Recreation Leadership.
    Harrisburg, PA   17110

Phone: 717-780-2531
Degrees: A 20/6,000
Options: RL, TR

The Pennsylvania State University
College of Agriculture
Dr. Harry L. Mosher, Program Leader
Forest Technology
Mont Alto, PA 17237

Phone: 717-749-3111
Degrees: A - -/826
Options: G2, FR

VIRGINIA

J. Sargeant Reynolds Community College
Math and Science Division
Recreation Leadership Tech.
Robert J. Moseley II, Head
P.O. Box 12084
Richmond, VA 23241

Phone: 804-264-3367
Degrees: A 30/9,100
Options: G1

Tidewater Community College
Technologies
James A. Cutchins
Recreation Leadership
1700 College Crescent
Virginia Beach, VA 23456

Phone: 804-427-3070
Degrees: A 45/8,500
Options: G1

WASHINGTON

Bellevue Community College
    H.P.E.R.
    Lynn E. Sanford, Chair
    Recreation Leadership
    300 Landerholm Circle, SE
    Bellevue, WA 98007

    Phone: 206-641-2353
    Degrees: A 60/10,000
    Options: G1, G2, G3, CA, CO, CE, ER, LE,
    MM, MU, OC, OE, OR, PM, RA, RL, SR, SS, TR,
    TT, VY, UR

Centralia College
    Bob Reiner
    H.P.E.R.
    600 W. Locust
    Centralia, WA 98531

    Phone: 206-736-9391
    Degrees: A -/1,500
    Options: G1

Everett Community College
    P.E.R.
    D. L. Whitchurch, Director
    Leisure Studies
    801 Wetmore
    Everett, WA 98201

    Phone: 206-259-7151, Ext. 325
    Degrees: A 15/4,000+
    Options: CA, OC, RL, TR

Fort Steilacoom Community College
    Richard S. Firman
    Dept. of Recreation, Parks, & Leisure
    Services

9401 Farwest Dr., SW
Tacoma, WA 98498

Phone: 206-964-6721
Degrees: A C 60/3,500
Options: Gl, G2, CA, CR, CO, ER, FM, MU,
PM, RL, SS, TR, TT, VY

Green River Community College
    Cris Miller, Coordinator
    Recreation Leadership
    12401 SE 320th
    Auburn, WA 98002

    Phone: 206-833-9111
    Degrees: A 35/4,000
    Options: Gl

Walla Walla Community College
    Prog. in Recreation Leadership
    John Volek
    500 Taysich Way
    Walla Walla, WA 99362

    Phone: 509-527-4310
    Degrees: A 20/4,000
    Options : CA, CI, FR, LE, OE, OR, PM, PP,
    RL, SR, VY

Wenatchee Valley College
    P.E. Dept.
    J. Kalahar, Chairman
    Outdoor Recreation
    1300 Fifth St.
    Wenatchee, WA 98801

    Phone: 509-662-1651, Ext. 243
    Degrees: A C -/1,800
    Options: Gl, G3, CA, CO, LE, OE, OR

WISCONSIN

University of Wisconsin, Whitewater
    H.P.E.R.
    George Arimond, Coordinator
    Recreation and Leisure Minor
    134 William Center
    Whitewater, WI   53190

    Phone: 414-473-1140
    Degrees: Minor 60/10,000
    Options: Gl, CI, CO, MU, OR, SR, TR

WYOMING

Northwest Community College
    Division of Life and Health Science
    Ken Rochlite, Director
    Recreation and Leisure Studies
    Powell, WY   82435

    Phone: 307-754-2066
    Degrees: A -/800
    Options: Gl

CANADA

Fairview College
    Ken Rintoul, Coor.
    Box 3000
    Fairview, Alberta, Can.   T0H 1L0

Lakeland College
    Dept. of Human and Natural Resources
    Dr. Gordon Hills, Director
    Parks and Recreation Program
    Vermilion, Alberta, Can.   T0B 4M0

Phone: 403-853-2971
Degrees: C 15/450
Options: EI, FM, LE, OE, PM, PP

Lethbridge Community College
Natural and Social Sciences
Doug Alston
Recreation Management
Lethbridge, Alberta, Can. T1K 1L6

Phone: 403-320-3219
Degrees: A 50/1,800
Options: FM, MU, RA

Mount Royal College
Dept. of Leisure Services and P.E.
Tom Wright, Acting Chairman
Leisure Services
4825 Richard Rd., SW
Calgary, Alberta, Can. T3A 1S7

Phone: 403-240-6509
Degrees: Diploma 75/5,347
Options: LE, TR

Craiboo College
Dept. of Social Sciences
Neville Flanagan, Coordinator
Leisure and Recreation Mgmt.
Box 3010
Kamloops, B.C., Can. V2C 5N3

Phone: 604-374-0123
Degrees: C 30/1,500
Options: G1, FM, RA, TR

Malaspina College
Social Science Area
Mr. E. Sutherland, Coordinator
Leisure Studies

900 - 5th St.
Nanaimo, British Columbia, Can.

Phone: 604-753-3245
Degrees: A 40/7,000
Options: Gl, MU, RL, TR, TT

Canadore College of Applied Arts and Technology
     Applied Arts Dept.
     George Follis, Coordinator
     Program in Recreation Leadership
     P.O. Box 5001
     North Bay, Ontario, Can. P1B 8K9

     Phone: 705-474-7600, Ext. 2119
     Degrees: A 72/1,800
     Options: FM, RA, RL, TR

Confederation College
     Marlene Lindsay, Coordinator
     Recreational Leadership Program
     Box 398
     Thunder Bay, Ontario, Can P7C 4W1

     Phone: 807-475-6252
     Degrees: C 56/-
      Options: Gl, CE, FM, MU, OC, OR, RA, RL,
     TR, VY

Humber College of Applied Arts and Technology
     Applied Arts Division
     Mr. J. A. Bowman
     Recreation Leadership Program
     205 Humber College Blvd.
     Rexdale, Ontario, Can. M9W 5L7

     Phone: 416-675-3111, Ext. 493
     Degrees: C 125/8,500
     Options: Gl, MU, OE, OR, RA, RL

Mohawk College
    Faculty of Applied Arts
    L. Stanbridge, Chairman
    Dept. of Recreation and Leisure Studies
    P.O. Box 2034
    Hamilton, Ontario, Can., L0R 2B0

    Phone: 416-389-4461
    Degrees: C 100/4,100
    Options: CA, CE, FM, LE, MU, OC, OR, TR

College de Riviere-du-Loup
    Dept. Techniques de Loisirs
    Richard Boutet, Coordonnateur
    Dept. Techniques de Loisirs
    80, Rue Frontenac
    Riviere-du-Loup, Quebec, Can. G5R 1S8

    Phone: 418-862-6903
    Degrees: Diploma   Etudes   Collegiales
    250/1800
    Options: Gl

Dawson College
    Viger Campus
    A Ross Seaman, Chairman
    Community Recreation Leadership
    535 Viger St.
    Montreal, Quebec, Can.

    Phone: 514-849-2551
    Degrees: Diploma 96/1,800
    Options: Gl, CI, MU, OE, OR, RA, RL, VY

MASTER'S DEGREES

ALABAMA
  University of South Alabama, Mobile

ARIZONA
  Arizona State University, Tempe
  University of Arizona, Tuscon

ARKANSAS
  University of Arkansas, Fayetteville

CALIFORNIA
  California State University
      Fresno
      Sacramento
      Chico
      Los Angeles
      Northridge
      Long Beach
  San Diego State University, San Diego
  San Francisco State University, S.F.
  San Jose State University, San Jose
  University of the Pacific, Stockton
  University of Southern California

COLORADO
  Colorado State University, Ft. Collins
  University of Colorado, Boulder
  University of Northern Colorado, Greeley

CONNECTICUT
  Central Conn. State College, New Britain
  Southern Connecticut University, New Haven
  University of Connecticut, Storrs

FLORIDA
  Florida International University, Miami
  Florida State University, Tallahassee
  University of West Florida, Pensacola

GEORGIA
Georgia Southern College, Statesboro
University of Georgia, Athens

IDAHO
University of Idaho, Moscow

ILLINOIS
Chicago State University, Chicago
George Williams University, Downers Grove
Illinois State University, Normal
Southern Illinois University, Carbondale
University of Illinois, Champaign
Western Illinois University, Macomb

INDIANA
Ball State University, Muncie
Butler University, Indianapolis
De Pauw University, Greencastle
Indiana University, Bloomington
Purdue University, West Lafayette

IOWA
Iowa State University, Ames
Drake University, Des Moines
University of Iowa, Iowa City

KANSAS
Kansas State University, Manhatten
Pittsburg State University, Pittsburg
University of Kansas, Lawrence

KENTUCKY
Eastern Kentucky University, Richmond
Morehead State University, Morehead
University of Kentucky, Lexington
Western Kentucky University, Bowling Green

LOUISIANA
Louisiana State University, Baton Rouge

Southern University and A&M College, Baton Rouge

MAINE
University of Maine, Orono

MARYLAND
University of Maryland, College Park

MASSACHUSETTS
Boston University, Boston
Bridgewater State College, Bridgewater
Northeastern University, Boston
Springfield College, Springfield

MICHIGAN
Central Michigan University, Mt. Pleasant
Michigan State University, East Lansing
Northern Michigan University, Marquette
University of Michigan, Ann Arbor
Wayne State University, Detroit

MINNESOTA
University of Minnesota, Minneapolis
University of Minnesota - Twin Cities, St. Paul

MISSISSIPPI
University of Southern Mississippi, Hattiesburg

MISSOURI
Central Missouri State University Warrensburg
University of Missouri, Columbia

MONTANA
Montana State University, Bozeman
University of Montana, Missoula

NEBRASKA
   Chadrom State College, Chadrom
   University of Nebraska, Lincoln
   University of Nebraska, Omaha

NEW HAMPSHIRE
   University of New Hampshire, Durham

NEW JERSEY
   Fairleigh Dickinson University, Madison

NEW MEXICO
   University of New Mexico, Albuquerque

NEW YORK
   New York University, New York
   State University of New York, Cortland

NORTH CAROLINA
   North Carolina State University, Raleigh
   University of North Carolina, Chapel Hill
   University of North Carolina, Greensboro

NORTH DAKOTA
   University of North Dakota, Grand Forks

OHIO
   Bowling Green State University, Bowling
   Green
   Kent State University, Kent
   Miami University of Ohio, Oxford
   Ohio State University, Columbus
   University of Akron, Akron
   University of Toledo, Toledo

OKLAHOMA
   Oklahoma State University, Stillwater
   Southwestern Oklahoma State University,
   Weatherford
   University of Oklahoma, Norman

University of Tulsa, Tulsa

OREGON
  Oregon State University, Corvallis
  University of Oregon, Eugene

PENNSYLVANIA
  Penn State University, University Park
  Slippery Rock University, Slippery Rock
  Temple University, Philadelphia

SOUTH CAROLINA
  Clemson University, Clemson

SOUTH DAKOTA
  University of South Dakota, Vermillion

TENNESSEE
  Memphis State University, Memphis
  University of Tennessee, Knoxville

TEXAS
  North Texas State University, Denton
  Texas A&M University, College Station
  Texas Tech. University, Lubbock
  Texas Women's University, Denton

UTAH
  Brigham Young University, Provo
  University of Utah, Salt Lake City
  Utah State University, Logan

VERMONT
  University of Vermont, Burlington

VIRGINIA
  George Mason University, Fairfax
  Bradford University, Bradford
  Virginia Commonwealth University, Richmond
  Virginia Tech., Blacksburg

WASHINGTON
    Central Washington University, Ellensburg
    Eastern Washington University, Cheney
    University of Washington, Seattle

WASHINGTON, D.C.
    George Washington University
    Howard University

WEST VIRGINIA
    West Virginia University, Morgantown

WISCONSIN
    University of Wisconsin, La Crosse
    University of Wisconsin, Madison

WYOMING
    University of Wyoming, Laramie

CANADA
    Dalhousie University, Halifax, Nova Scotia
    Lake Head University, Thunder Bay, Ontario
    University of Alberta, Edmonton

DIRECTORATE DEGREES

CONNECTICUT
    University of Connecticut, Storrs

GEORGIA
    University of Georgia, Athens

IOWA
    Iowa State University, Ames

INDIANA
    Indiana University, Bloomington

KENTUCKY
    University of Kentucky, Lexington

MASSACHUSETTS
    Boston University, Boston

MISSOURI
    University of Missouri, Columbus

DOCTORATE DEGREES

ARIZONA
    University of Arizona, Tuscon

CALIFORNIA
    University   of   Southern   California,   Los
    Angeles

COLORADO
    Colorado State University, Ft. Collins

CONNECTICUT
    University of Connecticut, Storrs

GEORGIA
    University of Georgia, Athens

IDAHO
    University of Idaho, Moscow

ILLINOIS
    University of Illinois, Champaign

INDIANA
    Ball State University, Muncie
    Indiana University, Bloomington
    Purdue University, West Lafayette

MAINE
    University of Maine, Orono

MARYLAND
    University of Maryland, College Park

MASSACHUSETTS
     Boston University, Boston

MICHIGAN
     Michigan State University, East Lansing
     University of Michigan, Ann Arbor

MINNESOTA
     University of Minnesota, Minneapolis
     University of Minnesota-Twin Cities, St.
     Paul

NEBRASKA
     University of Nebraska, Lincoln

NEW MEXICO
     University of New Mexico, Albuquerque

NEW YORK
     New York University, New York

NORTH CAROLINA
     University of North Carolina, Greensboro

OKLAHOMA
     Oklahoma State University, Stillwater

OREGON
     University of Oregon, Eugene

PENNSYLVANIA
     Penn State University, University Park
     Temple University, Philadelphia

TEXAS
     North Texas State University, Denton
     Texas A&M University, College Station
     Texas Women's University, Denton

UTAH
University of Utah, Salt Lake City
Utah State University, Logan

VIRGINIA
Virginia Tech. University, Blacksburg

WASHINGTON
University of Washington, Seattle

WISCONSIN
University of Wisconsin, Madison
University of Wisconsin, Milwaukee

GENERAL RECREATION PROGRAMS

For this and all following sections on emphasis
the Associate Degree schools have been
omitted from the listing.

ARIZONA
Northern Arizona University, Flagstaff

ARKANSAS
University of Arkansas, Fayetteville

CALIFORNIA
California State University, Hayward
California State University, Long Beach
California State University, Dominquez
Hills, Carson
California Poly State University, San Luis
Obispo
Chapman College, Orange
Humboldt State University, Arcata
Pepperdine University, Malibu
San Francisco State University, S.F.
University of California, Davis
University of California, Riverside
University of La Verne, La Verne

Whittier College, Whittier

COLORADO
Adams State College, Alamosa

CONNECTICUT
University of Connecticut, Storrs

DELAWARE
University of Delaware, Newark

FLORIDA
Florida International University, Miami
University of Miami, Coral Gables
University of West Florida, Pensacola

GEORGIA
North Georgia College, Dahlonega

HAWAII
University of Hawaii, Honolulu

IDAHO
Northwest Nazarene College, Nampa
University of Idaho, Moscow

ILLINOIS
Chicago State University, Chicago
College of St. Francis, Joliet
Eastern Illinois University, Charleston
Elmhurst College, Elmhurst
Northeastern Illinois University, Chicago
Rockford College, Rockford

INDIANA
Anderson College, Anderson
Butler University, Indianapolis
Huntington College, Huntington
Indiana State University, Evansville
Indiana University, Bloomington

Taylor University, Upland

IOWA

Drake University, Des Moines
Graceland College, Lamoni
Iowa State University, Ames
University of Iowa, Iowa City
Wartburg College, Waverly

KANSAS

Bethany College, Lindsborg
Emporia State University, Emporia

KENTUCKY

Western Kentucky University, Bowling Green

MAINE

Unity College, Unity

MARYLAND

Hood College, Frederick

MASSACHUSETTS

Bridgewater State, Bridgewater

MICHIGAN

Calvin College, Grand Rapids
Eastern Michigan University, Ypsilanti
Grand Valley State College, Allendale
Hope College, Holland
Western Michigan University, Kalamazoo

MINNESOTA

Bemidji State University, Bemidji
St. Cloud State University, St. Cloud
Winona State University, Winona

MISSISSIPPI

Alcorn State University, Lorman

MISSOURI
>   Central Missouri State University,
>   Warrensburg
>   Southeastern Missouri State University,
>   Cape Girardeau

MONTANA
>   Montana State University, Bozeman

NEBRASKA
>   Chadrum State College, Chadrum
>   Kearney State College, Kearney
>   Wayne State College, Wayne

NEVADA
>   University of Nevada, Las Vegas

NEW MEXICO
>   Eastern New Mexico University, Portales
>   New Mexico Highlands University, Las Vegas

NEW YORK
>   Long Island University, Green Vale

NORTH CAROLINA
>   Belmont Abbey College, Belmont
>   University of North Carolina, Chapel Hill
>   Wingate College, Wingate

NORTH DAKOTA
>   North Dakota State University, Fargo

OHIO
>   Central State University, Wilberforce
>   Ohio University, Athens

OKLAHOMA
>   Oral Roberts University, Tulsa
>   Southwestern Oklahoma State University,
>   Weatherford

University of Oklahoma, Norman

OREGON
    Oregon State University, Corvallis
    Pacific University, Forest Grove
    University of Oregon, Eugene

PENNSYLVANIA
    Cheney State College, Cheney
    Messiah College, Grantham

SOUTH CAROLINA
    Benedict College, Columbia

SOUTH DAKOTA
    Yankton College, Yankton

TENNESSEE
    University of Tennessee, Knoxville

TEXAS
    Baylor University, Waco
    North Texas State University, Denton
    Southwest Texas State University, San
    Marcos
    Texas Christian University, Ft. Worth
    Texas Tech. University, Lubbock

UTAH
    Utah State University, Logan

VERMONT
    Green Mountain College, Poultney

VIRGINIA
    Ferrum College, Ferrum
    Lynchburg College, Lynchburg

WASHINGTON
    Central Washington University, Ellensburg

Pacific Lutheran University, Tacoma
Washington State University, Pullman
Western Washington University, Bellingham

WISCONSIN
University of Wisconsin, Whitewater

WYOMING
University of Wyoming, Laramie

CANADA
Red Deer College, Red Deer, Alberta
University of New Brunswick, Fredericton
Confederation College, Thunder Bay, Ontario
Concordia University, Montreal, Quebec

GENERAL RESOURCE RELATED PROGRAMS

FLORIDA
Florida International University, Miami

GEORGIA
North Georgia College, Dahlonega

INDIANA
De Pauw University, Greencastle

LOUISIANA
Louisiana Tech. University, Rushton

MAINE
Unity College, Unity

MINNESOTA
University of Minnesota, St. Paul

MISSOURI
Southeastern Missouri State University,
Cape Girardeau

NEW YORK
   Long Island University, Green Vale

OKLAHOMA
   Oklahoma State University, Stillwater

TEXAS
   Texas A&M University, College Station
   Texas Tech. University, Lubbock

VIRGINIA
   George Mason University, Fairfax

WASHINGTON
   Washington State University, Pullman

WEST VIRGINIA
   Shepherd College, Shepherdstown

WISCONSIN
   University of Wisconsin, River Falls

WYOMING
   University of Wyoming, Laramie

CANADA
   Lakehead University, Thunder Bay, Ontario

COMMERCIAL RECREATION PROGRAMS

ALABAMA
   University of South Alabama, Mobile

ARIZONA
   Arizona State University, Tempe
   Northern Arizona University, Flagstaff

CALIFORNIA
   California State Poly Tech, Pomona
   California State University, Chico

California State University, Hayward
California State University, Northridge
San Francisco State University, S.F.
San Jose State University, San Jose
University of California, Davis
University of the Pacific, Stockton

COLORADO
Colorado State University, Ft. Collins
University of Colorado, Boulder

CONNECTICUT
Southern Connecticut University, New Haven

GEORGIA
Georgia Southern College, Statesboro

IDAHO
University of Idaho, Moscow

ILLINOIS
Illinois State University, Normal
Southern Illinois University, Carbondale
University of Illinois, Champaign

INDIANA
Purdue University, West Lafayette

KANSAS
Pittsburg State University, Pittsburg

KENTUCKY
Western Kentucky University, Bowling Green

MARYLAND
University of Maryland, College Park

MASSACHUSETTS
Springfield College, Springfield
University of Massachusetts, Amherst

MICHIGAN
    Central Michigan University, Mt. Pleasant
    Ferris State College, Big Rapids
    Michigan State University, East Lansing
    Western Michigan University, Kalamazoo

MINNESOTA
    University of Minnesota, Minneapolis

MISSISSIPPI
    Mississippi State University, Mississippi
    State

MISSOURI
    Missouri Western State College, St. Joseph
    Southwestern Missouri State College,
    Springfield
    University of Missouri, Columbia

NEBRASKA
    Kearny State College, Kearny
    University of Nebraska, Omaha

NEW JERSEY
    Fairleigh Dickenson University, Madison

NEW YORK
    Ithaca College, Ithaca
    Long Island University, Green Vale
    State University of New York, Brockport

NORTH CAROLINA
    East Carolina University, Greenville
    Elon College, Elon
    North Carolina State University, Raleigh
    University of North Carolina, Greensboro
    University of North Carolina, Wilmington

OHIO
    Bowling Green State University, Bowling
    Green
    University of Toledo, Toledo

PENNSYLVANIA
    East Stroudsburg State College, East
    Stroudsburg
    Penn State University, University Park

TEXAS
    Texas A&M University, College Station

UTAH
    University of Utah, Salt Lake City
    Utah State University, Logan

VERMONT
    Johnson State College, Johnson
    Norwich University, Northfield
    University of Vermont, Burlington

VIRGINIA
    Marymount College of Virginia, Arlington
    Old Dominion University, Norfolk
    Virginia Commonwealth University, Richmond

WASHINGTON
    Eastern Washington University, Cheney
    Washington State University, Pullman

WISCONSIN
    University of Wisconsin, Madison
    University of Wisconsin, Whitewater

WYOMING
    University of Wyoming, Laramie

FOREST RECREATION PROGRAMS

CALIFORNIA
    University of California, Davis

COLORADO
    Colorado State University, Ft. Collins

IDAHO
    University of Idaho, Moscow

ILLINOIS
    Southern Illinois University, Carbondale

INDIANA
    Purdue University, West Lafayette

IOWA
    Iowa State University, Ames

KENTUCKY
    University of Kentucky, Lexington

LOUISIANA
    Louisiana Tech University, Rushton

MAINE
    University of Maine, Orono

MASSACHUSETTS
    Springfield College, Springfield

MICHIGAN
    Ferris State College, Big Rapids

MINNESOTA
    University of Minnesota, St. Paul

MISSOURI
    University of Missouri, Columbia

MONTANA
University of Montana, Missoula

NEW YORK
Long Island University, Green Vale

NORTH CAROLINA
North Carolina State University, Raleigh

OKLAHOMA
Oklahoma State University, Stillwater

OREGON
Oregon State University, Corvallis

TENNESSEE
University of Tennessee, Knoxville

TEXAS
Texas A&M University, College Station

UTAH
Utah State University, Logan

VERMONT
University of Vermont, Burlington

VIRGINIA
Virginia Tech, Blacksburg

WASHINGTON
University of Washington, Seattle

WEST VIRGINIA
West Virginia University, Morgantown

WISCONSIN
University of Wisconsin, Madison

MUNICIPAL RECREATION AND PARKS PROGRAMS

ALABAMA
    University of Alabama, University
    University of South Alabama, Mobile

ARIZONA
    Arizona State University, Tempe
    Northern Arizona University, Flagstaff

ARKANSAS
    Arkansas Tech University, Russellive

CALIFORNIA
    San Francisco State University, S.F.
    San Jose State University, San Jose
    University of California, Davis
    University of the Pacific, Stockton
    University of Southern California, Los
    Angeles
    Whittier College, Whittier

COLORADO
    Mesa College, Grand Junction
    University of Northern Colorado, Greeley

CONNECTICUT
    University of Connecticut, Storrs

FLORIDA
    University of Florida, Gainesville

GEORGIA
    Georgia Southern College, Statesboro
    University of Georgia, Athens

ILLINOIS
    George Williams College, Downers Grove
    Western Illinois University, Macomb

INDIANA
Indiana University, Bloomington
Purdue University, West Lafayette

IOWA
Drake University, Des Moines

KANSAS
Kansas State University, Manhatten
University of Kansas, Lawrence

KENTUCKY
Eastern Kentucky University, Richmond
University of Kentucky, Lexington
Western Kentucky University, Bowling Green

LOUISIANA
Louisiana State University, Baton Rouge

MARYLAND
Hood College, Frederick

MASSACHUSETTS
Springfield College, Springfield
University of Massachusetts, Amherst

MICHIGAN
Ferris State College, Big Rapids
Northern Michigan University, Marquette
Wayne State University, Detroit
Western Michigan University, Kalamazoo

MINNESOTA
University of Minnesota, Minneapolis

MISSISSIPPI
Mississippi State University, Mississippi
State
University of Southern Mississippi
Hattiesburg

MISSOURI
     Central Missouri State University
     Warrensburg
     Missouri Western State College, St. Joseph
     Southwest Missouri State University,
     Springfield

MONTANA
     University of Montana, Missoula

NEBRASKA
     University of Nebraska, Omaha

NEW JERSEY
     Fairleigh Dickinson College, Madison

NEW YORK
     Long Island University, Green Vale

NORTH CAROLINA
     East Carolina University, Greenville
     Elon College, Elon
     North Carolina State University, Raleigh
     Univerity of North Carolina, Greensboro
     Western Carolina University, Cullowhee

OHIO
     Bowling Green State University, Bowling
     Green
     Central State University, Wilberforce
     Kent State University, Kent
     Ohio University, Athens

OKLAHOMA
     Southwestern Oklahoma State University,
     Weatherford
     University of Tulsa, Tulsa

PENNSYLVANIA
     Penn State University, University Park

Temple University, Philadelphia

SOUTH DAKOTA
Yankton College, Yankton

TENNESSEE
University of Tennessee, Knoxville

TEXAS
Texas A&M University, College Station
Texas Tech University, Lubbock

UTAH
University of Utah, Salt Lake City

VERMONT
Johnson State College, Johnson

VIRGINIA
Radford University, Radford
Virginia Commonwealth University, Richmond
Virginia Tech Univerity, Blacksburg

WASHINGTON
Eastern Washington University, Cheney
Washington State University, Pullman

WEST VIRGINIA
West Virginia University, Morgantown

WISCONSIN
University of Wisconsin, Madison
University of Wisconsin, Milwaukee
University of Wisconsin, River Falls
University of Wisconsin, Whitewater

WYOMING
University of Wyoming, Laramie

CANADA

> Red Deer College, Red Deer, Alberta
> Dalhousie University, Halifax, Nova Scotia
> Confederation College, Thunder Bay, Ontario
> Mohawk College, Hamilton, Ontario

OUTDOOR RECREATION PROGRAMS

ALABAMA

> University of South Alabama, Mobile

CALIFORNIA

> California State Poly Tech, Pomona
> California State University, Hayward
> California State University, Northridge
> Humboldt State University, Arcada
> San Diego State University, San Diego
> San Francisco State University, S.F.
> University of California, Davis
> University of California, Riverside

COLORADO

> Colorado State University, Ft. Collins
> University of Colorado, Boulder
> University of Northern Colorado, Greeley

CONNECTICUT

> Southern Connecticut University, New Haven

GEORGIA

> Georgia Southern College, Statesboro
> University of Georgia, Athens

ILLINOIS

> Chicago State University, Chicago
> George Williams College, Downers Grove
> Southern Illinois University, Carbondale
> University of Illinois, Champaign
> Western Illinois University, Macomb

INDIANA
Ball State University, Muncie
Butler University, Indianapolis
Huntington College, Huntington
Indiana University, Bloomington

IOWA
Iowa State University, Ames

KANSAS
University of Kansas, Lawrence

KENTUCKY
University of Louisville, Louisville
Western Kentucky University, Bowling Green

MAINE
Unity College, Unity

MARYLAND
Hood College, Frederick

MASSACHUSETTS
Bridgewater State College, Bridgewater
Springfield College, Springfield
University of Massachusetts, Amherst

MICHIGAN
Central Michigan University, Mt. Pleasant
Michigan State University, East Lansing
Northern Michigan University, Marquette
University of Michigan, Ann Arbor
Wayne State University, Detroit

MINNESOTA
Winona State University, Winona

MISSISSIPPI
University of Southern Mississippi,
Hattiesburg

MISSOURI
Southwest Missouri State University,
Springfield
University of Missouri, Columbia

MONTANA
University of Montana, Missoula

NEBRASKA
Nebraska Wesleyan University, Lincoln
University of Nebraska, Omaha

NEW YORK
Ithaca College, Ithaca
Long Island University, Green Vale
State University of New York, Cortland

NORTH CAROLINA
Appalachian State University, Boone
North Carolina State University, Raleigh
University of North Carolina, Wilmington

OHIO
Bowling Green State University, Bowling
Green
Kent State University, Kent
Miami University, Oxford
Ohio State University, Columbus
Ohio University, Athens

OKLAHOMA
Oklahoma State University, Stillwater
Oral Roberts University, Tulsa
Southwestern Oklahoma University,
Weatherford
University of Oklahoma, Norman

OREGON
Oregon State University, Corvallis
University of Oregon, Eugene

PENNSYLVANIA
    Penn State University, University Park

SOUTH DAKOTA
    South Dakota State University, Brookings
    University of South Dakota, Vermillion

TENNESSEE
    Memphis State University, Memphis
    Middle Tennessee State University,
    Murfeesboro

TEXAS
    Texas A&M University, College Station

UTAH
    Brigham Young University, Provo
    Utah State University, Logan

VERMONT
    Lindon State College, Lindonville
    Norwich University, Northfield
    University of Vermont, Burlington

VIRGINIA
    Old Dominion University, Norfolk
    Radford University, Radford
    Virginia Tech, Blacksburg

WASHINGTON
    Eastern Washington University, Cheney
    University of Washington, Seattle

WASHINGTON, D.C.
    Howard University

WISCONSIN
    Northland College, Ashland
    University of Wisconsin, Madison
    University of Wisconsin, Whitewater

WYOMING
   University of Wyoming, Laramie

CANADA
   Red Deer College, Red Deer, Alberta
   University of Alberta, Edmonton
   University of Manitoba, Winnipeg, Manitoba
   Dalhousie University, Halifax, Nova Scotia
   Confederation College, Thunder Bay, Ontario
   Mohawk College, Hamilton, Ontario

PARK AND RESOURCE MANAGEMENT PROGRAMS

ALABAMA
   Auburn University, Auburn
   University of Alabama, University
   University of South Alabama, Mobile

ARIZONA
   Arizona State University, Tempe
   University of Arizona, Tucson

CALIFORNIA
   California State University, Sacramento
   California State University, Chico
   Pacific Union College, Angwin
   San Jose State University, San Jose
   University of California, Davis

COLORADO
   Colorado State University, Ft. Collins

DELAWARE
   University of Delaware, Newark

IDAHO
   University of Idaho, Moscow

ILLINOIS
   Southern Illinois University, Carbondale

Western Illinois University, Macomb

INDIANA
Purdue University, West Lafayette

KENTUCKY
Eastern Kentucky University, Richmond

MAINE
University of Maine, Orono

MASSACHUSETTS
Springfield College, Springfield
University of Massachusetts, Amherst

MICHIGAN
Ferris State College, Big Rapids
Michigan State University, East Lansing
Western Michigan University, Kalamazoo

MINNESOTA
University of Minnesota, St. Paul

MISSISSIPPI
University of Southern Mississippi,
Hattiesburg

MONTANA
University of Montana, Missoula

NEW HAMPSHIRE
University of New Hampshire, Durham

NEW MEXICO
University of New Mexico, Albuquerque

NEW YORK
Long Island University, Green Vale

NORTH CAROLINA
    East Carolina University, Greenville
    North Carolina State University, Raleigh
    University of North Carolina, Greensboro

OHIO
    University of Toledo, Toledo

OKLAHOMA
    University of Oklahoma, Norman

OREGON
    Oregon State University, Corvallis

SOUTH CAROLINA
    Clemson University, Clemson

SOUTH DAKOTA
    South Dakota State University, Brookings
    University of South Dakota, Vermillion

TENNESSEE
    University of Tennessee, Knoxville

TEXAS
    Texas A&M University, College Station
    Texas Tech University, Lubbock

UTAH
    University of Utah, Salt Lake City
    Utah State University, Logan

VIRGINIA
    Virginia Commonwealth University, Richmond
    Virginia Tech, Blacksburg

WASHINGTON
    Eastern Washington University, Cheney
    Washington State University, Pullman

WASHINGTON, D.C.
     Howard University

WEST VIRGINIA
     West Virginia University, Morgantown

WISCONSIN
     University of Wisconsin, La Crosse
     University of Wisconsin, Madison
     University of Wisconsin, River Falls

WYOMING
     University of Wyoming, Laramie

CANADA
     University of Alberta, Edmonton, Alberta

RECREATION ADMINISTRATION PROGRAMS

ALABAMA
     Auburn University, Auburn
     University of South Alabama, Mobile

ARKANSAS
     Arkansas Tech University, Russellive

CALIFORNIA
     California State University, Fresno
     California State University, Los Angeles
     California State University, Sacramento
     California Poly State University, San Luis
     Obispo
     Humboldt State University, Arcada
     Pacific Union College, Angwin
     San Diego State University, San Diego
     San Jose State University, San Jose
     University of California, Davis
     University of Southern California, Los
     Angeles

COLORADO
>   Colorado State University, Ft. Collins
>   University of Northern Colorado, Greeley

CONNECTICUT
>   Southern Connecticut University, New Haven
>   University of Connecticut, Storrs

FLORIDA
>   Florida State University, Tallahassee
>   University of Florida, Gainesville

GEORGIA
>   University of Georgia, Athens

IDAHO
>   University of Idaho, Moscow

ILLINOIS
>   Chicago State University, Chicago
>   College of St. Francis, Joliet
>   Elmhurst College, Elmhurst
>   George Williams College, Dowers Grove
>   University of Illinois, Champaign
>   Western Illinois University, Macomb

INDIANA
>   Huntington College, Huntington
>   Indiana State University, Terre Haute
>   Indiana University, Bloomington
>   Purdue University, West Lafayette

IOWA
>   Drake University, Des Moines
>   Iowa State University, Ames
>   University of Iowa, Iowa City

KANSAS
>   Kansas State University, Manhatten
>   Pittsburg State University, Pittsburg

University of Kansas, Lawrence

KENTUCKY
Eastern Kentucky University, Richmond

LOUISIANA
Southern University and A&M College, Baton
Rouge

MARYLAND
University of Maryland, College Park

MASSACHUSETTS
Northeastern University, Boston
Springfield College, Springfield
University of Massachusetts, Amherst

MICHIGAN
Ferris State College, Big Rapids
Michigan State University, East Lansing
Wayne State University, Detroit
Western Michigan University, Kalamazoo

MINNESOTA
Bemidji State University, Bemidji
St. Cloud State University, St. Cloud
University of Minnesota, Minneapolis
Winona State University, Winona

MISSISSIPPI
Mississippi State University, Mississippi
State
University   of   Southern   Mississippi,
Hattiesburg

MISSOURI
Central Missouri State University,
Warrensburg
University of Missouri, Columbia

MONTANA
    University of Montana, Missoula

NEBRASKA
    Nebraska Wesleyan University, Lincoln

NEW HAMPSHIRE
    University of New Hampsire, Durham

NEW JERSEY
    Fairleigh Dickenson University, Madison

NEW MEXICO
    University of New Mexico, Albuquerque

NEW YORK
    Long Island University, Green Vale
    New York University, New York

NORTH CAROLINA
    Appalachian State University, Boone
    Belmont Abbey College, Belmont
    Elon College, Elon
    North Carolina State University, Raleigh
    University of North Carolina, Chapel Hill

NORTH DAKOTA
    University of North Dakota, Grand Forks
OHIO
    Bowling Green State University, Bowling
    Green
    Central State University, Wilberforce
    Miami University, Oxford

OKLAHOMA
    Oklahoma State University, Stillwater
    Southwestern Oklahoma University,
    Weatherford
    University of Oklahoma, Norman

OREGON
University of Oregon, Eugene

PENNSYLVANIA
Penn State University, University Park
Temple University, Philadephia

SOUTH CAROLINA
Benedict College, Columbia

SOUTH DAKOTA
University of South Dakota, Vermillion
Yankton College, Yankton

TENNESSEE
Memphis State University, Memphis
University of Tennessee, Knoxville

TEXAS
Le Tourneau College, Long View
North Texas State University, Denton
Texas A&M University, College Station
Texas Women's University, Denton

UTAH
Brigham Young University, Provo
Utah State University, Logan

VERMONT
Lindon State College, Lindonville
Norwich University, Northfield

VIRGINIA
Old Dominion University, Norfolk
Radford University, Radford
Virginia Commonwealth University, Richmond

WASHINGTON
Eastern Washington University, Cheney

WASHINGTON, D.C.
    Howard University

WEST VIRGINIA
    West Virginia State College, Institute
    West Virginia University, Morgantown

WISCONSIN
    University of Wisconsin, Madison

WYOMING
    University of Wyoming, Laramie

CANADA
    Red Deer College, Red Deer, Alberta
    University of Alberta, Edmonton
    University of British Columbia, Vancouver
    University of Manitoba, Winnipeg
    Dalhousie University, Halifax, Nova Scotia
    Confederation University, Thunder Bay,
    Ontario

THERAPEUTIC RECREATION PROGRAMS

ALABAMA
    University of Alabama, University
    University of South Alabama, Mobile

ARIZONA
    Arizona State University, Tempe
    Northern Arizona University, Flagstaff

CALIFORNIA
    California Poly State University, San Luis
    Obispo
    California State Poly Tech, Pomona
    California State University, Chico
    California State University, Dominguez
    Hills, Carson
    California State University, Fresno

California State University, Hayward
California State University, Los Angeles
California State University, Northridge
California State University, Sacramento
Pacific Union College, Angwin
San Diego State University, San Diego
San Francisco State University, S.F.
San Jose State University, San Jose
University of the Pacific, Stockton

COLORADO
Mesa College, Grand Junction
University of Colorado, Boulder
University of Northern Colorado, Greeley

CONNECTICUT
Southern Connecticut University, New Haven

FLORIDA
Florida State University, Tallahassee
University of Florida, Gainesville

GEORGIA
Georgia Southern, Statesboro
University of Georgia, Athens

IDAHO
University of Idaho, Moscow

ILLINOIS
Chicago State University, Chicago
College of St. Francis, Julliet
Eastern Illinois University, Charleston
Southern Illinois University, Carbondale
University of Illinois, Champaign

INDIANA
Huntington College, Huntington
Indiana State University, Terre Haute
Indiana University, Bloomington

IOWA

    Drake University, Des Moines
    Iowa State University, Ames
    University of Iowa, Iowa City
    University of Northern Iowa, Cedar Falls

KANSAS

    Kansas State University, Manhatten
    Pittsburg State University, Pittsburg
    University of Kansas, Lawrence

KENTUCKY

    University of Kentucky, Lexington
    Western Kentucky University, Bowling Green

LOUISIANA

    Southern University and A&M College, Baton
    Rouge

MARYLAND

    Hood College, Frederick
    University of Maryland, College Park

MASSACHUSETTS

    Boston University, Boston
    Bridgewater State University, Bridgewater
    Northeastern University, Boston
    Springfield College, Springfield

MICHIGAN

    Central Michigan University, Mt. Pleasant
    Eastern Michigan University, Ypsilanti
    Grand Valley State College, Allendale
    Michigan State University, East Lansing
    University of Michigan, Ann Arbor
    Wayne State University, Detroit

MINNESOTA

    St. Cloud State University, St. Cloud
    University of Minnesota, Minneapolis

Winona State University, Winona

MISSISSIPPI
University of Southern Mississippi,
Hattiesburg

MISSOURI
Central Missouri State University,
Warrensburg
Missouri Western State College, St. Joseph
Northwest   Missouri   State   University,
Maryville
Southwest   Missouri   State   University,
Springfield
University of Missouri, Columbia

NEBRASKA
Nebraska Wesleyan University, Lincoln
University of Nebraska, Omaha

NEW HAMPSHIRE
University of New Hampshire, Durham

NEW JERSEY
Fairleigh Dickinson University, Madison

NEW MEXICO
University of New Mexico, Albuquerque

NEW YORK
Ithaca College, Ithaca
Long Island University, Green Vale
New York University, New York
St. Joseph's College, Patchoque
State University of New York, Brockport
State University of New York, Cortland

NORTH CAROLINA
East Carolina University, Greenville
University of North Carolina, Chapel Hill

University of North Carolina, Greensboro
University of North Carolina, Wilmington
Western Carolina University, Cullowhee

NORTH DAKOTA
University of North Dakota, Grand Forks

OHIO
Central State University, Wilberforce
Kent State University, Kent
Ohio State University, Columbus
Ohio University, Athens
University of Toledo, Toledo

OKLAHOMA
Oklahoma State University, Stillwater
Oral Roberts University, Tulsa
Southwestern Oklahoma State University, Weatherford
University of Oklahoma, Norman
University of Tulsa, Tulsa

OREGON
Pacific University, Forest Grove
University of Oregon, Eugene

PENNSLYVANIA
Cheney State College, Cheney
Penn State University, University Park
Slippery Rock University, Slippery Rock
Temple University, Philadelphia

SOUTH CAROLINA
Benedict College, Columbia
Clemson University, Clemson

SOUTH DAKOTA
University of South Dakota, Vermillion

TENNESSEE
>   Memphis State University, Memphis
>   Middle Tennessee State University,
>   Murfreesboro
>   University of Tennessee, Knoxville

TEXAS
>   North Texas State University, Denton
>   Texas Tech University, Lubbock
>   Texas Women's University, Denton

UTAH
>   Brigham Young University, Provo
>   University of Utah, Salt Lake City

VERMONT
>   Green Mountain College, Poultney
>   Lindon State College, Lindonville

VIRGINIA
>   Longwood College, Farmville
>   Old Dominion University, Norfolk
>   Radford College, Radford
>   Shenendoah College, Winchester
>   Virginia Commonwealth University, Richmond
>   Virginia Tech, Blacksburg

WASHINGTON
>   Eastern Washington University, Cheney
>   Pacific Lutheran University, Tacoma
>   Washington State University, Pullman

WASHINGTON, D.C.
>   George Washington University
>   Howard University

WEST VIRGINIA
>   Alderson-Broaddus College, Philippi
>   Marshall University, Huntington
>   West Virginia State College, Institute

West Virginia University, Morgantown

WISCONSIN
University of Wisconsin, Green Bay
University of Wisconsin, La Crosse
University of Wisconsin, Madison
University of Wisconsin, Milwaukee
University of Wisconsin, Whitewater

CANADA
Red Deer College, Red Deer, Alberta
University of Alberta, Edmonton
University of British Columbia, Vancouver
University of Manitoba, Winnipeg
Dalhousie University, Halifax, Nova Scotia
Confederation College, Thunder Bay, Ontario
Mohawk College, Hamilton, Ontario

TRAVEL AND TOURISM PROGRAMS

ALABAMA
University of South Alabama, Mobile

ARIZONA
Arizona State University, Tempe

CALIFORNIA
University of California, Davis
University of the Pacific, Stockton

COLORADO
Mesa College, Grand Junction

GEORGIA
Georgia Southern College, Statesboro

ILLINOIS
Illinois State University, Normal

INDIANA
    Purdue University, West Lafayette

MASSACHUSETTS
    Springfield College, Springfield

MICHIGAN
    Michigan State University, East Lansing

NEW HAMPSHIRE
    University of New Hampshire, Durham

NEW JERSEY
    Fairleigh Dickinson University, Madison

NEW YORK
    Long Island University, Green Vale

NORTH CAROLINA
    North Carolina State University, Raleigh
    University of North Carolina, Greensboro

OREGON
    University of Oregon, Eugene

PENNSLYVANIA
    Penn State University, University Park

SOUTH CAROLINA
    Clemson University, Clemson

TEXAS
    Texas A&M University, College Station

UTAH
    Utah State University, Logan

VERMONT
    Johnson State College, Johnson
    University of Vermont, Burlington

VIRGINIA
     Virginia Commonwealth University, Richmond

WASHINGTON, D.C.
     George Washington University

WISCONSIN
     University of Wisconsin, Madison

WYOMING
     University of Wyoming, Laramie

OTHER DEGREE PROGRAMS REPORTED

Children's Play and Development
Recreation Fitness
Leisure Studies
Community Recreation
Wilderness Management
Dance
Recreation Program
Human Services
Urban Forestry
Community Recreation
Corporate Fitness
Employee Industrial
Sport and Fitness
Public/Quasi Public
Wilderness Skills
Park and Recreation Administration
Community Leisure Services
Leisure Service Management
Fitness Supervision
Marine Coastal Recreation
Management
Physical Fitness Program and Administration
Hotel/Hospitality
Ski Area Management
Cultural Historical Resources

Indiana University, School of Health, Physical Education and Recreation, Department of Recreation and Park Administration, Bloomington, Indiana 47405. Dr. Theodore Deppe, Chairman.

The Department of Recreation and Park Administration is organized into six major divisions, each guided by a student-faculty advisory committee and a coordinator or director. These include: Graduate Studies, Leisure Research Institute, Undergraduate Studies, Continuing Education/Community Services, Professional Field Work and Placement Services, Bradford Woods Outdoor Education/Camping Center.

Undergraduate Curriculum: B.S. in Recreation with emphases in public parks and recreation, outdoor recreation, recreation leadership and programming, and therapeutic recreation.

Graduate Curriculum: M.S. (Master of Science) in Recreation, Re.Dir. (Director of Recreation), Re.D. (Doctor of Recreation), and Ph.D. in Leisure Behavior, a degree specifically designed to prepare candidates for research careers. Graduate options are available in park and recreation administration, therapeutic recreation, outdoor recreation and recreational sports administration.

UNIVERSITY
of
FLORIDA

DEPARTMENT OF RECREATION

Accreditation by the NRPA-AALR Council
on accreditation for public recreation
programs, and therapeutic recreation
programs.

INSTRUCTIONAL STAFF (1982-83)

Varnes, P. R., Chairman; Beland, R., Advisor
and Assistant Professor; Gamble, D., Advisor
and Assistant Professor; Gustke, L. D., Assistant Professor; Hall, L. T., Advisor and Associate Professor; Leilich, R. E., Professor;
McCall, G. E., Associate Professor; Regna,
J. L., Associate Professor; Williams, C. S.,
Associate Professor and Director of Campus
Recreation.

TENTATIVE SUMMER COURSES INCLUDE:

Philosophy and History of Recreation
Leadership and Social Recreation
Evaluation of Leisure Services
Seminar in Leisure Services
Leisure Education and Counseling
Variable Topics in Leisure Services

FOR MORE INFORMATION CONTACT:

Academic Advisement Office
Room 229 Florida Gym
University of Florida
Gainesville, Florida 32611
(904) 392-1910

UNIVERSITY OF ILLINOIS AT URBANA-CHAMPAIGN
(Accredited by the NRPA/AALR Council on Accreditation to October, 1983)

Location and
Mailing Address:

Dr. Joseph J. Bannon, Professor and Head of Department
Department of Leisure Studies
College of Applied Life Studies
1206 South Fourth Street, Room 104 Huff Gymnasium
University of Illinois at Urbana-Champaign
Champaign, Illinois 61820
217-333-4410

Curriculum Information:

Title:
Degrees Offered:

Department of Leisure Studies
B.S. in Leisure Studies; M.S. in Leisure Studies; and
Ph.D. with specialization in Leisure Studies

Program Emphases or Options:

Undergraduate students are prepared for mid-management
roles in recreation in a variety of agencies by pursu-
ing one of the following program options: program
management, therapeutic recreation, outdoor recreation
planning and management. Graduate students are prepared
for roles as teaching and research scholars and for
upper-level management positions. Master's degree
students may specialize in the following options: recreation and park administration, therapeutic recreation,
outdoor recreation and leisure behavior research.
Doctoral students may specialize in the study of leisure
behavior or the delivery of leisure services.

Research Division:
Leisure Behavior Research
    Lab

This laboratory is the organized research unit of the
Department and is located in the Institute for Child
Behavior and Development. The primary research objectives are to acquire knowledge about: (a) leisure
behavior from social-psychological and sociological
perspectives, and (b) play and movement behavior of
children and adults in leisure time activities. The
laboratory also studies leisure of the handicapped and
other special populations. Current research includes
program-oriented projects sponsored by government
agencies. The laboratory's faculty teach undergraduate
and graduate research courses and advise master's
and doctoral research projects.

Extension and Continuing
Education Activities:
Office of Recreation
and Park Resources

This unit is operated in conjunction with the Cooperative Extension Service, College of Agriculture. The
major purposes of the office are to assist Cooperative
Extension Service in conducting educational programs
to provide consultant services to governmental and
private agencies that involve unique problems in
recreation and parks; to strengthen teaching in the
department, to provide a laboratory for carrying out
sound recreation and park research programs, and to
communicate research findings to the field.

Prerequisites for Admission:

Undergraduate: Illinois resident/combination of rank
in high school class and admission test score. Out-of-
state/upper quarter of high school class. Graduate:
M.S./4.0 (in 5.0 system) grade point average for last
60 hours and acceptable test scores on GRE. Ph.D./mini-
mum 4.0 (in 5.0 system) grade point average for last 60
hours of undergraduate work and all graduate work and
acceptable test scores on GRE plus interview.

DEPARTMENT OF RECREATION AND LEISURE STUDIES

Indiana State University

Terre Haute, Indiana

47809

Degrees Offered

The Department of Recreation and Leisure Studies, School of Health, Physical Education and Recreation offers an accredited curriculum leading to a Bachelor of Science Degree in Recreation and Leisure Studies. The degree consists of 124 hours of coursework that includes 16 hours of practicum work in recreation agencies in a variety of community settings.

Accreditation

The Recreation and Leisure Studies curriculum is accredited by the NRPA/AALR Council on Accreditation to March, 1986, for Leisure Experiences for Special Populations, Leisure Services Management, Outdoor Education and Camp Leadership/Administration.

Prerequisites for Admission

Unconditional admission to Indiana High School graduates who rank in the upper 70% of their class; conditional admission for those who rank in the lower 30% of their class. Out-of-state high school graduates;unconditional admission for those who rank in the upper half of their class; conditional admission for those who rank at or below the 49th percentile, but above the 29th percentile.

Graduate Program

Indiana State University will offer a graduate program leading to the Master of Science in Recreation and Leisure Studies beginning with the fall semester, 1984. The Master of Science program will offer options of study in Management, Special Populations, and Outdoor Recreation.

The University Community

Indiana State University is located in Terre Haute, a city 70 miles southwest of Indianapolis. Terre Haute has an estimated metro-politan population of 115,000 and has numerous public and private recreation facilities nearby. The city and county departments of parks and recreation operate and maintain some of the finest parks in Indiana. The Department of Recreation and Leisure Studies operates and maintains a 70 acre outdoor learning laboratory provid-ing outdoor learning experiences for university students as well as or more than 3,000 elementary students annually.

DEPARTMENT OF RECREATION
2367 PERH BUILDING

University of Maryland
COLLEGE PARK, MD 20742
301-454-5621

Bachelor of Science

Master of Arts

Doctor of Philosophy

RECREATION AND LEISURE STUDIES
NRPA/AALR ACCREDITED IN:

OUTDOOR -
NATURAL AND HISTORICAL INTERPRETIVE SERVICES,
WATER, LAND, AND WILDLIFE RESOURCES MANAGE-
MENT, REGIONAL AND SITE FACILITIES PLANNING

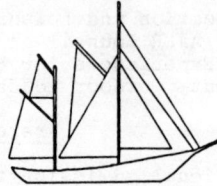

PROGRAM SERVICES -
COMMERCIAL, TOURISM, COMMUNITY ADMINISTRATION, CORRECTIONAL, EMPLOYEE
AND INDUSTRIAL RECREATION SERVICES; PROGRAM SPECIALTY AREAS (MUSIC,
DANCE, ETC.), PROGRAM DEVELOPMENT AND EVALUATION, ARTS, SPORTS AND
FITNESS MANAGEMENT

THERAPEUTIC -
PROGRAM PLANNING AND SERVICES FOR: THE AGING, MENTALLY RETARDED,
PHYSICALLY DISABLED, AND EMOTIONALLY DISTURBED, IN CLINICAL OR
COMMUNITY SETTINGS

A GOLD MINE
DEGREE PROGRAMS ARE INDIVIDUALLY
PLANNED, THE FACULTY IS LARGE, AND
MANY ARE NATIONALLY AND INTER-
NATIONALLY RECOGNIZED; CLASSES ARE SMALL
AS ARE STUDENT/FACULTY RATIOS. LOCATED IN
THE BALTIMORE-WASHINGTON CORRIDOR, OPPORTU-
NITIES FOR STUDY, EXPERIENCES AND PLAY,
WITHIN A 50 MILE RADIUS, ARE AMONG THE RICHEST
IN THE WORLD. EXAMPLES OF RESOURCES WITHIN 30 MINUTES
ARE THE LIBRARY OF CONGRESS, NATIONAL INSTITUTES OF
HEALTH, ALL U.S. GOVERNMENT DEPARTMENTS, STATE AND
REGIONAL COMMISSIONS, FORESTS, PARKS, THE CHESAPEAKE
BAY AND SUGARLOAF MOUNTAIN

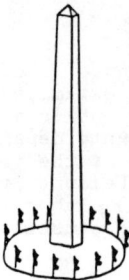

UNIVERSITY OF MISSOURI-COLUMBIA

Department of Recreation and Park Administration

General Information

The University of Missouri, Department of Recreation and Park Administration was established in 1966. It is one of approximately 30 programs accredited by the Council on Accreditation of National Recreation and Park Association/American Association for Leisure and Recreation. The department offers excellent opportunities in research, training and scholarship through various grants. The extension program offers service, continuing education and consultation to the state.

Bachelors Degree Requirements

- 132 credit hours including a 12 credit hour internship
- Minimum GPA of 2.0 in Recreation and Park Administration courses
- Selection of at least one of three areas of emphasis which include Therapeutic Recreation, Leisure Service Management, and Park Programs and Operation

Masters Degree Requirements

- A minimum of 37 credit hours with a maximum of 12 credit hours in research, problems, and readings
- Completion of a thesis or special problem
- Minimum GPA of 3.0
- Selection of an area of emphasis from Therapeutic Recreation, Tourism, Leisure Service Management, and Outdoor Recreation

Financial Aid Information

- Scholarships are available from the Missouri Park and Recreation Association and other soures to both undergraduate students (approximately $3,500 in 1982-83)
- Graduate assistantships are available to qualified applicants (approximately $87,359 in 1982-83)

Features and Unique Learning Opportunities at MIZZOU

- Microcomputer laboratory and skilled faculty to conduct training
- Diverse opportunities for a 12 credit hour internship (undergraduate)
- National scholastic honorary society chapter
- Affiliation with the Missouri Park and Recreation Association
- Second largest number of medical/rehabilitation facilities in the nation
- Job opportunities in tourism, commercial and public recreation management, and therapeutic recreation

For Further Information Write:

Dr. David M. Compton, Chairman
Department of Recreation and Park Administration
601 Clark Hall
University of Missouri
Columbia, Missouri 65211

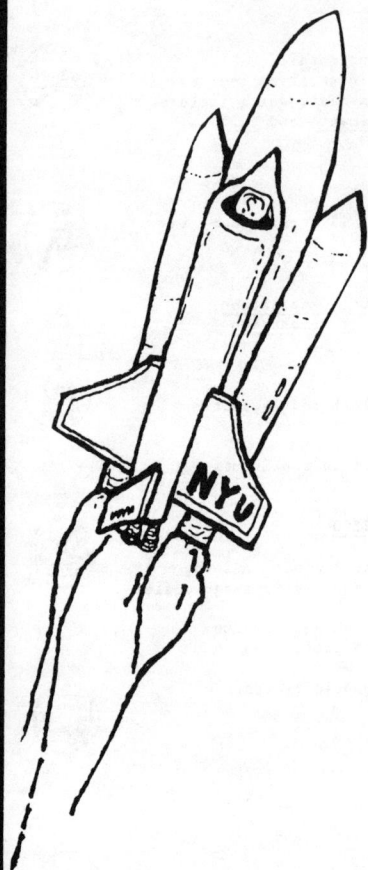

DEPARTMENT OF PARKS, RECREATION, AND TOURISM MANAGEMENT

College of Forest and Recreation Resources
Clemson University
267 Lehotsky Hall
Clemson, SC 29631
Telephone: (803)656-3036

DEGREES:

Bachelor of Science Degree
w/emphases
Community Leisure Services
Recreation Resource Management
Therapeutic Recreation
Travel and Tourism

Master of Recreation and Park Administration

Master of Science

FACULTY:

R. H. Becker, PhD	University of Maryland
G. R. Boettner, MEd	East Carolina University
H. Brantley, PhD	University of North Carolina
G. W. Burnett, PhD	University of Oklahoma
R. A. Conover, PhD	Colorado State University
L. W. Gahan, PhD	University of Illinois
H. J. Grove, MEd	Pennsylvania State University
G. E. Howard, PhD	University of Michigan
R. L. Howell, MURP	Virginia Commonwealth University
A. E. James, PhD	University of New Mexico
C. P. Kriese, MA	Tennessee Technological University
G. K. McLellan, PhD	University of Maryland
R. W. McLellan, PhD	University of Minnesota
F. A. McGuire, PhD	University of Illinois
B. J. Mihalik, PhD	Temple University
J. R. Pope, EdD	University of South Carolina
J. L. Stevenson, PhD	Indiana University
H. A. Thomas, MS	University of North Carolina
B. E. Trent, MEd	Springfield College
C. R. White, Jr., MS	Indiana University
M. H. Wynn, MS	Springfield College

Clemson University is a land-grant, state-supported university, fully accredited by the Southern Association of Colleges and Schools.

THE UNIVERSITY OF UTAH

DEPARTMENT OF RECREATION AND LEISURE
CHAIR: DR. L. DALE CRUSE, PROFESSOR
HPER N-226   (801) 581-8547 - 8542
SALT LAKE CITY, UTAH 84112

The University of Utah is located in the Great Salt Lake
Valley on the east bench of the Wasatch Mountains. Salt
Lake City provides an area with mountains, lakes, and
streams, within a few minutes of campus. There are five
National Parks, 43 State Parks and several outdoor recreation areas. Recreation agencies/hospitals/institu-
tions provide numerous resources. There are eight major
hospitals, mental health and correctional institutions,
divisional offices of National Park Service, B.L.M.,
and U.S. Forest Service. There are nine major ski resorts,
amusement parks, tennis courts, golf courses, and sports
malls. State, county, city, and recreation exists in an
area close to high mountain wilderness and/or desert
solitude.

B.S., M.S., Ed.D., and Ph.D. offered in Commercial (8 -
courses), Therapeutic (9 courses), Community (9 courses),
and Recreation Resource Management (9 courses). In addition, there are Core Courses for all areas. Fieldwork and
Internships are required.

Faculty: L. Dale Cruse, Professor/Chair, Taylor Ellis -
Commercial and Outdoor Recreation, George Fenstermacher-
Community and Therapeutic Recreation, Sydney Post - Thera-
peutic Recreation, Linn Rockwood-Community Recreation,
Norma Polovitz-Outdoor Recreation skill classes, and one
vacant position in the Outdoor and Commercial areas.
Part-time faculty: H. Goodro, Wilderness Survival and Out-
door Adventure, J. Burgon-Community Schools, S. Christian-
sen-Community Recreation, G. Swenson-Community Recreation,
T. Green-Outdoor/Commercial, R. Leake-Administration, R.
Ward-Therapeutic Recreation, R. Humphries-Law, and J.
Clift-Therapeutic Recreation.

FINANCIAL ASSISTANCE AVAILABLE--NRPA/AALR ACCREDITATION

Directory of College/University Programs in Recreation, Leisure Services and Resources 1981
Compiled and edited by Donald D. Henkel
Published by NRPA

This publication culminates the efforts of NRPA to computerize all known park and recreation curricula in colleges and universities throughout the United States and Canada. Approximately 500 separate programs are listed as compared with the previous listings of 315 in 1973 and 203 in 1969. The Directory is divided into two major sections. Section I is the most comprehensive and presents institutions in alphabetical order by state and province, name of department chair and title, department name and address and phone numbers. The second section lists all institutions by options or areas of specializations. Degree levels are identified. *1981, 48 pp.*   ***Cost:* $6.00**

Recreation, Park and Open Space Standards and Guidelines
Published by NRPA

The long-awaited "Recreation, Park and Open Space Standards and Guidelines," the first update issued in more than a decade, has been published by the National Recreation and Park Association to help communities identify and design facilities and park lands needed to meet recreation demand.

The document, three years in preparation, gives community planners model step-by-step methods for urban and rural park and recreation planning.

It offers guidelines on space requirements, location and service radius for such recreation facilities as sports courts and arenas, archery ranges, trails, beach areas, swimming pools, running tracks and youth sports fields, among others. The guidelines also indicate the number of facilities needed based on population.

The Standards and Guidelines do not establish an absolute level of park or open space land mandated to serve specific population levels. Rather, the document establishes methods by which individual communities can adequately plan their own facilities and spaces. *1983, 136 pp.*   ***Cost:* $25.00**

FROM
AA🚶R

THE AMERICAN ASSOCIATION FOR LEISURE AND RECREATION

LEISURE TODAY — SELECTED READINGS (VOL. II)

MORE THAN 60 ARTICLES FROM TODAY'S LEADERS IN
LEISURE AND RECREATION, PSYCHOLOGY, AND THE
SOCIAL SCIENCES, TOPICS INCLUDE LEISURE AND
AGING, HIGH ADVENTURE LEISURE PURSUITS AND
RISK RECREATION, THERAPEUTIC RECREATION,
LEISURE COUNSELING, COMMERCIAL RECREATION,
LEISURE THEORY AND PHILOSOPHY, POPULAR CULTURE
AND LEISURE EDUCATION. EDITED BY FRED W.
MARTIN. 1980. 160 pp. (0-88314-123-X)
PRICE: Nonmember $10.95. Member $9.86

LEISURE: NO ENEMY BUT IGNORANCE

THE FIVE J.B. NASH SCHOLARS PRESENT COMPLE-
MENTARY AND CONTROVERSIAL PERSPECTIVES ON THE
FUTURE OF LEISURE. A CHAPTER DEVOTED TO NASH'S
PHILOSOPHY ALSO IS INCLUDED. IDEAL AS A
SUPPLEMENTARY TEXT IN THE CLASSROOM OR A
VALUABLE ADDITION TO A PROFESSIONAL LIBRARY.
1983. 96 pp. (0-88314-244-9)
PRICE: Nonmember $10.45. Member $9.41

WHO'S WHERE IN RECREATION EDUCATION

A SOURCE DIRECTORY OF CURRICULA AND INSTI-
TUTIONS IN THE FIELD OF PARKS AND RECREA-
TION. IT'S USE AS A TELEPHONE/MAILING
DIRECTORY, GUIDE FOR PARK AND RECREATION
EDUCATION EXPLORATION AND SOURCE OF TREND
CHANGES IN TRAINING, CURRICULA, AND STUDENT
POPULATION IS INVALUABLE. DATA IS COMPILED
BY 4-YEAR INSTITUTIONS, COMMUNITY COLLEGES,
DEGREE PROGRAMS, AND CURRICULA OPTION.
EDITED BY E. TAYLOR ELLIS. 1983. 175 pp.
(0-88314-224-4)
PRICE: Nonmember $ 8.50. Member $7.75

ORDER FORM ON BACK

AALR PUBLICATIONS ORDER FORM

HOW TO ORDER

Use the convenient order form provided, (attach separate sheet if necessary) or institutional purchase order.

Mail order to: American Alliance Publications
P.O. Box 704
Waldorf, MD 20601

PAYMENT
Orders must be accompanied by payment or by official purchase order (institutions only). Visa/MasterCard may be used for orders of $10.00 or more.

DISCOUNT POLICY*
Orders for 10 or more copies of a single title are eligible for a 5% discount. No discount allowed on audiovisuals, fitness items and periodicals.

For information on dealer discounts, contact American Alliance Publication Sales.

SHIPPING AND HANDLING (All orders shipped UPS) Orders with check or money order uses the following chart to calculate your shipping charges and add these to your subtotal due.

Less than $10,00	= 1.50
$10.-$24.99	= 2.50
$25.-$49.99	= 3.50
$50.-$99.99	= 5.00
$100. or more	= 4% of total cost

Orders with VISA/MasterCard or Purchase Order, actual shipping will be added.

Phone Orders: (703) 476-3481

AAHPERD Order Form

Stock Number	Quantity	Title	Discount*	Cost

___ MEMBER   I.D. NO. _____
___ NONMEMBER

SUBTOTAL DUE $_____
SHIPPING CHARGES $_____
TOTAL ENCLOSED $_____

Method of Payment:
☐ Payment enclosed
☐ Master Charge ☐ VISA

(check type of card, add number and sign)

[| | | | | | | | | | | | | | | |] Signature of card holder   card expires

SHIP TO _____   BILL TO (institutional orders only) _____
ATTN _____   ATTN _____
ADDRESS _____   ADDRESS _____
CITY-STATE-ZIP CODE _____   CITY-STATE-ZIP CODE _____

Prices subject to change without notice.

AALR

The Leader in Leisure and Recreation...

The American Association for Leisure and Recreation (AALR) was formed in 1930 in response to growing public recognition of recreation as a fundamental human need. AALR's purpose is to develop and promote the organization of school, community and national leisure services and recreation education.

More than 7,000 student and professional members of AALR share a commitment to improve leisure lifestyles and recreational opportunities for all individuals. AALR provides you with the chance to help shape the leisure and recreation programs of our nation...while you shape your own professional future.

Serving Your Profession...

AALR
•Supports, encourages and provides guidance to members in the development and conduct of leisure services programs
•Encourages professional involvement and exchange
•Sponsors relevant programs at national and district conventions, workshops and conferences
•Aids in the development of quality recreation programs in schools
•Monitors recreation legislation and renders consultation at the request of legislators
•Provides opportunities for leadership and participation in committees, convention programs and special interest areas
•Disseminates information on topics of current interest in leisure and recreation
•Maintains liaisons with national and international organizations having similar concerns.

Helping You Grow as a Professional...

AALReporter

AALR's quarterly newspaper brings you scores of ideas and resources specifically relating to leisure and recreation including:
•job notices
•professional opportunities
•book reviews
•feature articles
•practical ideas for programming
•association news

The AALReporter welcomes member input, involvement and exchange.

Leisure Today

You receive two issues of *Leisure Today* each year. Each issue is coordinated by a different guest editor, who focuses on a current topic in leisure trends and offers a collection of perspectives from recognized experts. This special magazine is written for you, the professional in recreation, and comes to you as an insert in the *Journal of Physical Education, Recreation and Dance*.

Student Services

In addition to AAHPERDs Job Placement Service, AALR offers other attractive services to student members. A student representative is appointed to the AALR Board of Directors each year to ensure student input, and a section of the AALR Reporter is reserved for student exchange of ideas.

Information Referral Data Bank

AALR maintains an ever-growing referral file of information and organizations in the broad area of recreation and leisure services. If you need information, AALR will help you find it. AALR members also have access to AAHPERD's Unit of Programs for the Handicapped Information and Research Utilization Center in Physical Education and Recreation for the Handicapped.

Collegial Status

AALR members enjoy collegial status with the National Recreation and Park Association (NRPA) and the National Community Education Association (NCEA). AALR members are entitled to attend NRPA and NCEA conferences, conventions and workshops at member registration rates.

Professional Recognition

The AALR Awards recognize distinctive contributions in the fields of recreation and leisure. Specific awards focus on leadership, scholarship, and work with the handicapped.

Conventions and Conferences

National, state and local meetings give you the opportunity to meet your colleagues and hear outstanding speakers.

EASY STEPS TO
5 MEMBERSHIP
AMERICAN ALLIANCE FOR
HEALTH, PHYSICAL EDUCATION,
RECREATION AND DANCE

1 Yes, I want to join the **American Alliance.** Please start ☐ renew ☐ (check one) my membership.

Name _____

Address _____

City _____ State _____ Zip _____

2 ## I select membership in the following association(s) of the American Alliance

■ Check two boxes — you may check one association twice (Each check you make gives a portion of your dues to that association).

☐ ☐ American Association for Leisure and Recreation
☐ ☐ American School and Community Safety Association
☐ ☐ Association for the Advancement of Health Education
☐ ☐ Association for Research, Administration, Professional Councils and Societies
☐ ☐ National Association for Girls and Women in Sport
☐ ☐ National Association for Sports and Physical Education
☐ ☐ National Dance Association

3 Your **American Alliance** dues depend on your choice of periodicals.

Please: SELECT ONE OF THE OPTIONS BELOW;

Update and:	Professional	Graduate	Undergrad
Any one periodical	☐ $42	☐ $25	☐ $22.50
Any two periodicals	☐ $52	☐ $35	☐ $32.50
Any three periodicals	☐ $62	☐ $45	☐ $42.50

4 INDICATE THE PERIODICALS YOU WISH TO RECEIVE:
☑ Update
☐ Journal of Physical Education, Recreation and Dance
☐ Health Education
☐ Research Quarterly for Exercise and Sport

5 PLEASE CHECK ONE:
☐ My payment is enclosed (check payable to AAHPERD)
☐ I wish to charge my membership ☐ VISA ☐ MASTERCARD
Card # _____ Expiration Date _____
Signature _____

For office use only
DT: _____
Ck: _____   code
Amt. _____
No. _____

I understand that of the amount indicated for membership dues, $2.00 is for one year subscription to **UPDATE** and the following amounts are for the periodicals selected:

Research Quarterly - $6.00.
Health Education - $6.00.
and **JOPER** - $6.00

AAHPERD
1900 Association Drive,
Reston, Virginia 22091

⊙AAHPERD

AA⬛R

Do you have course work in:

- leisure services
- parks and resource management
- recreation programs/administration

If these courses lead to a certificate degree, please take the 5 minutes necessary to respond to this questionnaire. The results will be the basis of a Professional Preparation Directory which is projected for the following uses:

- Directory of institutions, departments, addresses, size of a program, accreditation, phone numbers
- A guide and resource for students and prospective students
- A resource for faculty in these related disciplines
- An updated mailing list for promotional purposes
- A list (not evaluated) of various emphases

Institution: _____

Do you offer classes in Leisure Services, Recreation Mgmt., Cultural Arts, etc.? ☐ Yes ☐ No

If not, please fill in name and mail.

Title of School/College where program is placed: _____

Unit: _____

Title and name of Admin. Head in Charge of Program (e.g., Chairman, Head, Associate Dean, etc): _____

_____

Title of Curriculum (e.g., Dept. of Leisure and Recreation Services; Program in Recreation Leadership; etc.):

_____

Address: _____

City: _____ State: _____ Zip: _____

Office Phone: (_____) _____ - _____

Enrollment On Your Campus in 1982: _____ ; Majors in Your Program—

Undergrad _____ Graduate _____ No Major/General Ed. Students _____

(OVER)

Level of Degrees Offered:

_____ Associate Arts   _____ Bachelors   _____ Doctorate
_____ Certificate Prog—Specify _____ _____ Masters   _____ None
          _____   _____ Directorate

Options or Areas of Emphasis (check those offered):

> For purposes of this form and the resulting directory: Option/Specialization or Area of Emphasis is loosely interpreted as
> ". . . a definitive area of study with several specialized courses complimenting a required core area of general
> park/recreation classes."

Some curricula do not have emphasis areas, therefore they train generalists, if so . . . check here:

_____ General Recreation Program (G1)
_____ General Resource Related Program (G2)
_____ General Cultural Arts (Music, Dance, etc.) Program (G3)

Emphasis Areas:

_____ Corrections (CX)   _____ Leisure Education (LE)   _____ Recreation Leadership (RL)
_____ Camping (CA)   _____ Marina/Aquatic Mgmt (MM)   _____ School Recreation (SR)
_____ Campus Rec/Intramurals (CI)   _____ Municipal Recreation/Parks   _____ Special Services (Armed
_____ Church Recreation (CR)   (MU)   Forces) (SS)
_____ College Union Mgt (CU)   _____ Older Citizens/Aging (OC)   _____ Therapeutic/Handicapped/
_____ Commercial Recreation (CO)   _____ Outdoor Education (OE)   Disabled (TR)
_____ Community School Ed (CE)   _____ Outdoor Recreation (OR)   _____ Travel/Tourism (TT)
_____ Employee Recreation (ER)   _____ Park/Resource Mgmt (PM)   _____ Urban/Innercity Recreation (UR)
_____ Environmental/Interpretive   _____ Park/Resource Planning (PP)   _____ Voluntary/Youth Service
          (EI)   _____ Research (RX)   Agencies (VY)
_____ Facility Maintenance (FM)   _____ Recreation Administration   _____ Other(s)—Specify _____
_____ Forest Recreation (FR)   (RA)   _____

1) If developing new programs, please list (by emphasis) and expected implementation date:

_____

_____

_____

2) Do you know of community colleges or universities in your state or region not well known in these fields? If so,
   please write down the institution and contact person for us to follow-up. Thank you!

          Institution/Address   Contact Person

_____   _____

_____   _____

_____   _____

_____   _____

AAHPERD

AA▮R

Do you have course work in:

- leisure services
- parks and resource management
- recreation programs/administration

If these courses lead to a certificate degree, please take the 5 minutes necessary to respond to this questionnaire. The results will be the basis of a Professional Preparation Directory which is projected for the following uses:

- Directory of institutions, departments, addresses, size of a program, accreditation, phone numbers
- A guide and resource for students and prospective students
- A resource for faculty in these related disciplines
- An updated mailing list for promotional purposes
- A list (not evaluated) of various emphases

Institution: _____

Do you offer classes in Leisure Services, Recreation Mgmt., Cultural Arts, etc.? ☐ Yes ☐ No

If not, please fill in name and mail.

Title of School/College where program is placed: _____

Unit: _____

Title and name of Admin. Head in Charge of Program (e.g., Chairman, Head, Associate Dean, etc): _____

_____

Title of Curriculum (e.g., Dept. of Leisure and Recreation Services; Program in Recreation Leadership; etc.):

_____

Address: _____

City: _____ State: _____ Zip: _____

Office Phone: (_____) _____-_____

Enrollment On Your Campus in 1982: _____ ; Majors in Your Program—

Undergrad _____ Graduate _____ No Major/General Ed. Students _____

(OVER)

Level of Degrees Offered:

_____ Associate Arts

_____ Certificate Prog—Specify _____

_____ Bachelors   _____ Doctorate
_____ Masters   _____ None
_____ Directorate

_____

Options or Areas of Emphasis (check those offered):

> For purposes of this form and the resulting directory: Option/Specialization or Area of Emphasis is loosely interpreted as ". . . a definitive area of study with several specialized courses complimenting a required core area of general park/recreation classes."

Some curricula do not have emphasis areas, therefore they train generalists, if so . . . check here:

_____ General Recreation Program (G1)
_____ General Resource Related Program (G2)
_____ General Cultural Arts (Music, Dance, etc.) Program (G3)

Emphasis Areas:

_____ Corrections (CX)
_____ Camping (CA)
_____ Campus Rec/Intramurals (CI)
_____ Church Recreation (CR)
_____ College Union Mgt (CU)
_____ Commercial Recreation (CO)
_____ Community School Ed (CE)
_____ Employee Recreation (ER)
_____ Environmental/Interpretive (EI)
_____ Facility Maintenance (FM)
_____ Forest Recreation (FR)

_____ Leisure Education (LE)
_____ Marina/Aquatic Mgmt (MM)
_____ Municipal Recreation/Parks (MU)
_____ Older Citizens/Aging (OC)
_____ Outdoor Education (OE)
_____ Outdoor Recreation (OR)
_____ Park/Resource Mgmt (PM)
_____ Park/Resource Planning (PP)
_____ Research (RX)
_____ Recreation Administration (RA)

_____ Recreation Leadership (RL)
_____ School Recreation (SR)
_____ Special Services (Armed Forces) (SS)
_____ Therapeutic/Handicapped/ Disabled (TR)
_____ Travel/Tourism (TT)
_____ Urban/Innercity Recreation (UR)
_____ Voluntary/Youth Service Agencies (VY)
_____ Other(s)—Specify _____

_____

1) If developing new programs, please list (by emphasis) and expected implementation date:

_____

_____

_____

2) Do you know of community colleges or universities in your state or region not well known in these fields? If so, please write down the institution and contact person for us to follow-up. Thank you!

Institution/Address   Contact Person

_____   _____

_____   _____

_____   _____

_____   _____

AAHPERD

AA⬛R

Do you have course work in:

- leisure services
- parks and resource management
- recreation programs/administration

If these courses lead to a certificate degree, please take the 5 minutes necessary to respond to this questionnaire. The results will be the basis of a Professional Preparation Directory which is projected for the following uses:

- Directory of institutions, departments, addresses, size of a program, accreditation, phone numbers
- A guide and resource for students and prospective students
- A resource for faculty in these related disciplines
- An updated mailing list for promotional purposes
- A list (not evaluated) of various emphases

Institution: _____

Do you offer classes in Leisure Services, Recreation Mgmt., Cultural Arts, etc.? ☐ Yes ☐ No

If not, please fill in name and mail.

Title of School/College where program is placed: _____

Unit: _____

Title and name of Admin. Head in Charge of Program (e.g., Chairman, Head, Associate Dean, etc): _____

_____

Title of Curriculum (e.g., Dept. of Leisure and Recreation Services; Program in Recreation Leadership; etc.):

_____

Address: _____

City: _____ State: _____ Zip: _____

Office Phone: (_____) _____ - _____

Enrollment On Your Campus in 1982: _____ ; Majors in Your Program—

Undergrad _____ Graduate _____ No Major/General Ed. Students _____

(OVER)

Level of Degrees Offered:

_____ Associate Arts
_____ Certificate Prog—Specify _____

_____ Bachelors   _____ Doctorate
_____ Masters   _____ None
_____ Directorate

_____

Options or Areas of Emphasis (check those offered):

> **For purposes of this form and the resulting directory: Option/Specialization or Area of Emphasis is loosely interpreted as ". . . a definitive area of study with several specialized courses complimenting a required core area of general park/recreation classes."**

Some curricula do not have emphasis areas, therefore they train generalists, if so . . . check here:

_____ General Recreation Program (G1)
_____ General Resource Related Program (G2)
_____ General Cultural Arts (Music, Dance, etc.) Program (G3)

Emphasis Areas:

_____ Corrections (CX)
_____ Camping (CA)
_____ Campus Rec/Intramurals (CI)
_____ Church Recreation (CR)
_____ College Union Mgt (CU)
_____ Commercial Recreation (CO)
_____ Community School Ed (CE)
_____ Employee Recreation (ER)
_____ Environmental/Interpretive (EI)
_____ Facility Maintenance (FM)
_____ Forest Recreation (FR)

_____ Leisure Education (LE)
_____ Marina/Aquatic Mgmt (MM)
_____ Municipal Recreation/Parks (MU)
_____ Older Citizens/Aging (OC)
_____ Outdoor Education (OE)
_____ Outdoor Recreation (OR)
_____ Park/Resource Mgmt (PM)
_____ Park/Resource Planning (PP)
_____ Research (RX)
_____ Recreation Administration (RA)

_____ Recreation Leadership (RL)
_____ School Recreation (SR)
_____ Special Services (Armed Forces) (SS)
_____ Therapeutic/Handicapped/Disabled (TR)
_____ Travel/Tourism (TT)
_____ Urban/Innercity Recreation (UR)
_____ Voluntary/Youth Service Agencies (VY)
_____ Other(s)—Specify _____

_____

1) If developing new programs, please list (by emphasis) and expected implementation date:

_____

_____

_____

2) Do you know of community colleges or universities in your state or region not well known in these fields? If so, please write down the institution and contact person for us to follow-up. Thank you!

Institution/Address   Contact Person

_____   _____

_____   _____

_____   _____

_____   _____